TUDOR TREASURES TO EMBROIDER

Pamela Warner

TUDOR TREASURES TO EMBROIDER

Pamela Warner

GUILD OF MASTER CRAFTSMAN PUBLICATIONS LTD

First published 2002 by
Guild of Master Craftsman Publications Ltd,
166 High Street, Lewes,
East Sussex, BN7 1XN

Text © Pamela Warner 2002
Copyright in the Work © Guild of Master Craftsman Publications Ltd

ISBN 1 86108 249 5

Cover and finished project photography by Christine Richardson
Design and cover design by Ian Hunt Design
Illustrations by John Yates from originals by Pamela Warner
Colour charts by Peter Rhodes from originals by Pamela Warner

Many thanks to Anne of Cleves Museum, Lewes, for kindly allowing us to use the
house for our location shoot.

Picture acknowledgements
Lindy Dunlop, page 89
Embroiderers' Guild, Hampton Court Palace, page 4
Julia Hedgecoe, page 7 (bottom)
V&A Picture Library, Victoria and Albert Museum, pages 5, 27, 67, 68, 69

Typeface: Berkeley and Trade Gothic

Colour origination by Viscan Graphics (Singapore)

Printed and bound by Sun Fung Offset Binding Co Ltd, China

Essentials

Projects

Appendix

CONTENTS

Note on Measurements

Throughout, measurements are given in both metric and imperial systems. *Please use only one system* for each project as the two are close alternatives only, not exact conversions.

Metric Conversion Table

Inches to millimetres

inches	mm	inches	mm	inches	mm
⅛	3	9	229	30	762
¼	6	10	254	31	787
⅜	10	11	279	32	813
½	13	12	305	33	838
⅝	16	13	330	34	864
¾	19	14	356	35	889
⅞	22	15	381	36	914
1	25	16	406	37	940
1¼	32	17	432	38	965
1½	38	18	457	39	991
1¾	44	19	483	40	1016
2	51	20	508	41	1041
2½	64	21	533	42	1067
3	76	22	559	43	1092
3½	89	23	584	44	1118
4	102	24	610	45	1143
4½	114	25	635	46	1168
5	127	26	660	47	1194
6	152	27	686	48	1219
7	178	28	711	49	1245
8	203	29	737	50	1270

Introduction to Tudor Treasures

The embroidery and design of the Tudor era, particularly during the reign of Elizabeth I, provide a rich and beautiful source for the projects presented within this book.

Many of the projects are based on exhibits from museum collections to retain the lively charm and authenticity of the period.

Counted thread techniques have been selected for the various projects, and are equally suited to embroiderers new to the craft and those with some experience.

The charts for each project are presented in colour. Clear diagrams show details and explain the step-by-step instructions. The charts can also be adapted for use on items other than those shown so that you may design your own unique items.

Influences on Design and Style

The Tudor period was a time of prosperity, reaching a height in the reign of Henry VIII. The arts blossomed and, by the reign of Elizabeth I, embroidery entered its second great period (the first era being that of 'opus anglicanum', the magnificent early church embroidery of the Middle Ages).

The Tudors

Date	Monarch
1485–1509	Henry VII
1509–1547	Henry VIII
1547–1553	Edward VI
1553–1553	Jane (ruled for nine days)
1553–1558	Mary I
1558–1603	Elizabeth I

The Stuarts

Date	Monarch
1603–1625	James I (VI Scotland)
1625–1649	Charles I
1649–1659	Commonwealth
1660–1685	Charles II
1685–1688	James II (VII Scotland)
1689–1701	William III and Mary II
1702–1714	Anne

Fig 1.1 A fragment, identified as either a coif or cover. English, late sixteenth century. Gift of John Jacoby. Photography by Julia Hedgecoe. © Embroiderer's Guild at Hampton Court Palace. The scrolling stem divides the design into compartments within which a selection of popular plants and insects have been stitched. The stem itself is worked in plaited braid stitch using metal thread. The coloured silks incorporate a range of surface stitches including buttonhole stitch, which has a raised effect. The background is filled in with tiny spangles: round discs of gilt metal, a forerunner of the modern sequin.

By the mid-sixteenth century, the houses of all but the very poor were more comfortable than earlier fortified dwellings. Internal staircases, fireplaces in every room and glazed windows contributed to an increased expectation of – and desire for – decoration in everyday living. The relative peace and affluence of the times allowed the wealthy to afford sumptuous furnishings and costume, providing an excellent opportunity for embroidery.

There was a great interest in the natural world: flowers, fruit, birds and insects – and in gardens, all of which were enthusiastically incorporated into designs by embroiderers of the time (see Figs 1.1 and 1.2).

Combinations of flowers of all kinds were used in a design, often framed within a scrolling stem, beautifully embroidered in fine, different-coloured

Fig 1.2 Detail of woman's linen jacket embroidered in black silk in a pattern of scrolling stems with leaves, flowers, birds and insects with chain, stem, satin, buttonhole and speckling stitches, English, 1620s.

Fig 1.3 Sketches of a
selection of embroidered
'slips' from items in the
Victoria and Albert
Museum and Traquair
House. The embroidery
would have been cut out
and applied to satin or
velvet and finished with
a couched outline.

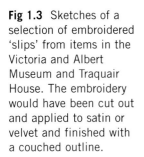

floss silks, using long and short, split and stem stitches. Some examples included raised stitches, adding a three-dimensional effect to petals or leaves, and many were embellished with metal threads (see Fig 1.5, facing opposite).

Engraved wood blocks were made to illustrate the books and herbals of the time. Full of plant illustrations, these provided a useful source for embroidery design. The designs were often used to create a 'slip': a single plant with bud, flower and often the fruit, which was embroidered, cut out and applied to fabric (see Fig 1.3). A slip is also a gardening term for a cutting. In the next chapter, I look again at the use of slips in embroidery of this period (see page 27). Some herbals exist showing pages which have been pricked through along the outlines of plants to enable an embroiderer to 'pounce' the design on to the fabric. 'Prick and pounce' is an old method of transferring a design, still in use today for intricate designs.

Cushions were widely used on chairs, benches and window seats – items which were not generally upholstered until the seventeenth century (see my interpretation, Fig 1.4). Canvaswork, which was extremely hard wearing, was used extensively, and embroidered with wool and silk threads. In addition to floral designs, narrative and pictorial subjects were popular for these items.

Blackwork was another widely used technique for decorating household items and costume, often worked in metal thread to enrich a piece. Details of this technique are given in the Beautiful Blackwork chapter, see page 67.

Fig 1.4 Cream and Green silk cushions (see pages 28 and 39).

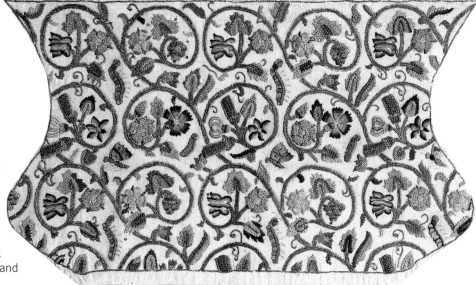

Fig 1.5 Coif panel. British, late sixteenth or early seventeenth century. Gift of Lady Mary Cayley. © Julia Hedgecoe. It is made of linen embroidered with silk thread, metal thread and silver spangles.

ESSENTIALS

Materials and Equipment

Fabrics

Canvas

Embroidery canvas is available in various 'counts': the number of threads per 2.5cm (1in). The higher the number of threads, the finer the canvas.

Single thread canvas, also known as mono canvas, has been used for the projects in this book. It is available in white, pale yellow or 'antique' brown.

Interlock canvas is white, with a twisted weave in one direction. It is more pliable than the normal weave and can be cut to shape without fraying. This canvas is used for most of the projects in Favourite Flowers, page 27 onwards.

Coin net is a cotton canvas with a 24 count and is sometimes available from retailers in different colours.

When working one of the charts, each square on the chart represents one stitch over one thread of the canvas.

Evenweave fabrics

Evenweave fabric has a regular weave with threads of the same thickness in both directions. The fabric can be of cotton or linen. It is also available in various counts.

Linen is the easiest of these fabrics to work on as the threads of the fabric are finer, providing a larger hole.

Cotton is a 'fluffier' thread in texture, and appears to be more densely woven as the holes are less defined.

When using one of the charts with an evenweave fabric, each square on the chart represents one stitch over two threads of the fabric.

Block weave fabrics

Hardanger and Aida fabrics have a weave pattern that forms blocks. Aida is available in many different counts and Hardanger from 18 to 22. With these, each square on one of the charts represents one stitch over one block.

Surface embroidery fabrics

Some of the projects in Fragrant Knot Gardens (see page 89 onwards) are worked in surface stitchery on plain fabrics. Any smooth lightweight fabric will be suitable for these projects: silk dupion or satin, cotton poplin or lawn, or a synthetic with similar qualities.

Frames

Using an embroidery frame

To help reduce distortion, most of the projects will benefit from being worked in an embroidery frame. It is also easier to count threads when the fabric is stabilized in a frame. There are various types to choose from and each requires a different method of preparation.

Slate frames

Refer to Fig 2.1. Slate frames are rectangular and consist of two sides with circular notches, into which two rounded sides with webbing are fixed. Wing nuts at each corner tension the fabric once rolled over the rounded sides.

Mounting the fabric

1 Dismantle the frame and lay the two webbing strips face down on two opposite sides of the fabric. Make sure the fabric is on the straight grain.
2 Stitch through the fabric and webbing in firm backstitch with a strong thread.
3 Locate the rounded sides into the notches in the square sides, and roll the fabric until the required tension is achieved. Tighten the wing nuts.
4 Lace the sides of the fabric and frame together with a strong thread.

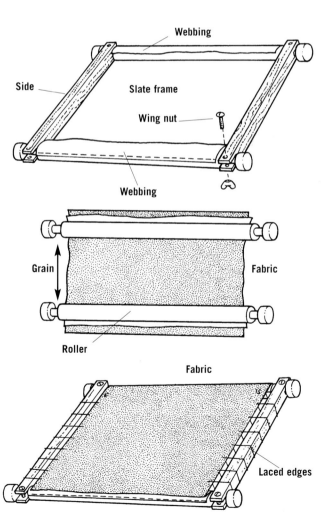

Fig 2.1 Mounting a piece of fabric onto a slate frame.

Fig 2.2 Mounting fabric
to a stretcher.

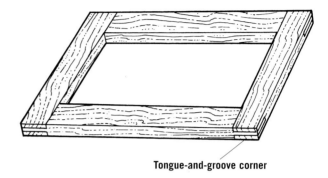

Tongue-and-groove corner

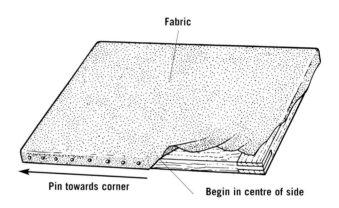

Fabric

Pin towards corner   Begin in centre of side

Stretchers

This is an easier frame which can be made with artist's stretchers, which are available in many sizes. The sides can be bought in pairs to the required length, with tongue-and-groove joints at the ends which simply slot together. Alternatively, a home-made version can be made with some softwood, utilizing angle brackets at the corners.

Mounting the fabric

1 Assemble the stretcher by pushing the ends together.
2 Refer to Fig 2.2. Using drawing pins or thumb tacks, pin the fabric along one of the longer sides to stretch the fabric slightly. Begin in the centre and work towards a corner. Return to the centre and complete the side towards the remaining corner.
3 Repeat with the opposite side, making sure the grain of the fabric is straight across the frame.
4 Pin the two remaining sides in the same way, checking the grain of the fabric as you go.

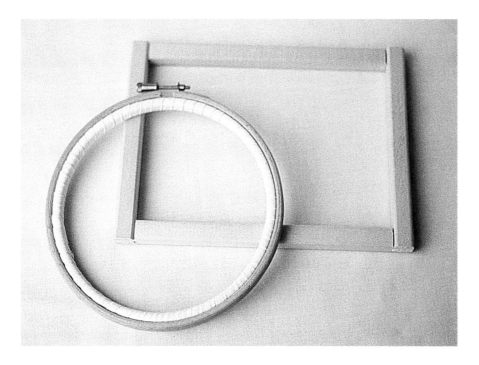

Fig 2.3 A tambour and a small stretcher.

Tambour or round embroidery frames

These frames are made in wood or plastic. The wooden ones are best as the fabric does not slip, especially if the inner ring is bound with binding, strips of fabric or tape (see Figs 2.3 and 2.4).

Mounting the fabric

1 Lay the inner ring down on a surface.
2 Position the fabric over the inner ring so that the area you want to work is central.
3 Push the outer ring down over the fabric and inner ring, pulling the fabric taut, and tighten the tension screw.

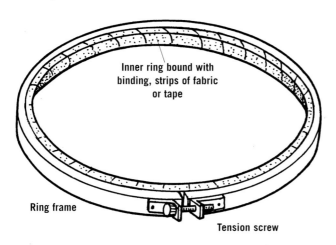

Fig 2.4 A tambour or round frame.

Inner ring bound with
binding, strips of fabric
or tape

Ring frame

Tension screw

Finishing
Techniques

Blocking embroidery

Counted thread embroidery on canvas or linen can distort with the tension of the stitches and you may need to 'block' the fabric back into shape.

Materials

Pinboard or similar (soft enough to take drawing pins or thumb tacks)

Paper

Transparent plastic sheeting

Drawing pins or thumb tacks

Waterproof pen

Working method

1 Draw a rectangle on the paper with the waterproof pen. The rectangle needs to be larger than the embroidery to provide straight lines for you to follow when pinning out the fabric/canvas.

2 Lay the paper on the pinboard and cover with the sheeting (see Fig 2.5).

3 Trim any excess fabric from around the embroidery, leaving 2.5cm (1in).

4 With a damp cloth or sponge, lightly dampen the embroidery and the surrounding canvas or linen.

5 Lay the embroidery within the rectangle drawn on the paper. Begin pinning the fabric to the board, from the middle of one side and working towards a corner. Gently stretch the fabric as you work along the sides, ensuring the grain of the fabric is straight.

6 Return to the middle of the side and complete to the remaining corner.

7 Repeat the process with the opposite side, beginning in the middle and making sure the grain of the fabric runs straight across the centre.

8 Complete the process with the two remaining sides.

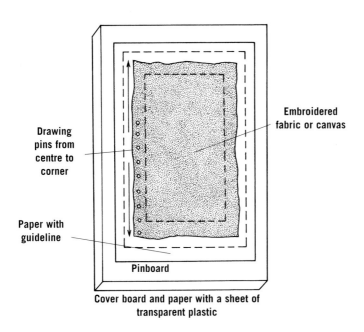

Fig 2.5 Blocking a completed piece of canvaswork.

Drawing
pins from
centre to
corner

Embroidered
fabric or canvas

Paper with
guideline

Pinboard

**Cover board and paper with a sheet of
transparent plastic**

9 Leave to dry naturally, laid flat in an even temperature.

10 Once completely dry, remove from the board.

Mitred corners

Working a mitred corner will help to cut down unnecessary bulk.

Working method

1 Trim the seam allowance.

2 Cut a small amount from the corner of the fabric (see Fig 2.6a).

3 Fold the corner down diagonally.

4 Fold the adjacent sides once, and then again to form a hem (see Fig 2.6b and c). Secure with tiny hemming stitches.

Fig 2.6 Making a mitred corner.

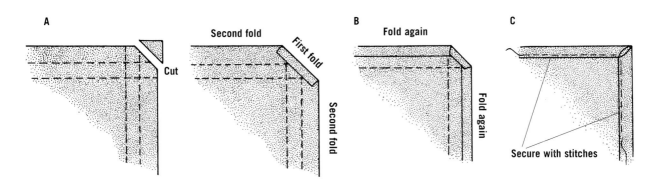

A

Cut

Second fold

First fold

Second fold

B

Fold again

Fold again

C

Secure with stitches

Mounting embroidery for framing

You will first need to purchase a picture frame or have one made.

Materials

Thick card or thin 3mm (⅛in) hardboard

Strong thread

Working method

1 Cut the piece of thick card or thin hardboard to fit into the rebate of the picture frame.

2 Make sure that all tacking stitches or guidance lines are removed from the embroidery.

3 Lay the embroidery right side down on a surface.

4 Position the piece of card or hardboard over the embroidery in the required position.

5 Using a large needle and a long length of strong thread, fasten on into the surplus fabric of one of the sides. It is a good idea to begin in the centre and work towards a corner.

6 Take a stitch into the opposite side into the surplus fabric.

7 Draw up to bring the surplus fabric around to the back of the picture.

8 Continue lacing from one side to the other. Return to the centre and complete the sides. Work along each stitch in turn, pulling the threads tight, and fasten off securely.

9 Trim some of the excess fabric from the corners.

10 Repeat the process with the remaining two sides.

Stitch Glossary

Advance knot

When you begin to stitch on canvas or evenweave fabrics it is not possible to darn in or use a double stitch. The best method is to begin with an advance knot.

Tie a knot in the end of the thread and take the needle through from the front of the work so that the knot is sitting on the front. This should be positioned about 10cm (4in) from the position of the first stitch.

Bring the needle and thread through to the right side ready for the first stitch and continue working.

When the thread or area of stitching is finished, look at the back of the work. If your stitching has incorporated the length of thread between the knot and your first stitch, you can simply cut the thread next to the stitching. If the stitching has not covered the thread, cut the knot off from the right side and insert the length of thread into a needle and fasten off into the back of the stitching.

Backstitch

This stitch is used to work a smooth line.

Bring the needle up through the fabric and take it down again to give the length of stitch required.

Bring the needle up through the fabric again, the length of a stitch away from the previous stitch (A).

Take the needle back through the fabric next to the previous stitch (B).

Once your backstitch is complete, fasten the end off into the back of the stitches.

Bullion knots

This is a knotted stitch that gives long knots instead of the round knots of the French knot.

Bring the needle up through the fabric and take a stitch the desired length of the knot, but do not pull the thread to flatten the resulting loop.

Use the loop to wind the thread around the needle enough times to cover the length of the knot.

Hold the twists around the needle firmly with the fingers and pull the thread through to draw the knot down onto the fabric.

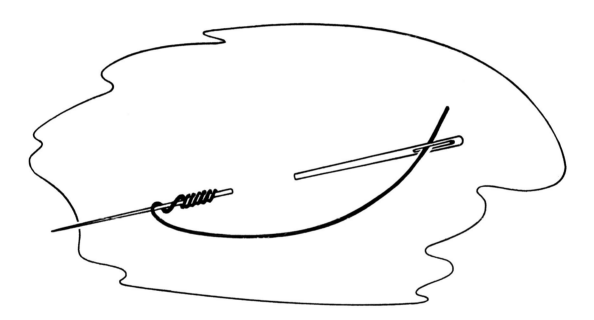

Couching

This method is used to lay a thread, or pair of threads, on the surface of the fabric, which is stitched down with a second finer thread.

The diagram shows a single thread for clarity but, when using metallic threads, two threads are laid side by side.

Place the thread or threads to be laid in position on the fabric, leaving about 5cm (2in) before the first stitch.

With another needle, bring the sewing thread through from the back immediately beside the laid thread or threads (A), and take a stitch over them (B). Continue to secure the laid thread in this manner, at the same time moving the laid thread, if necessary, to form the shape or line required. Fasten the sewing thread off behind the stitching.

Now take a large darning or tapestry needle and insert into the fabric at the point where the last stitch is required. Thread the ends of the laid metallic thread through the eye of the needle and pull through to the back. Repeat with the second laid thread if necessary.

Next, take the starting ends of the laid metallic thread through in the same manner.

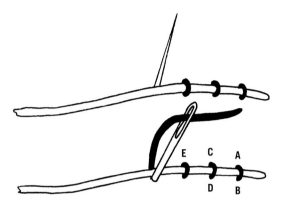

Cross stitch

The diagram (below) shows the method for working a row of cross stitch, by making the first half of the stitch all the way along the row and then working the second half of the stitch on the way back along the row.

For the first row, bring the needle up at A, down at B, up at C, down at D, and so on, until the row is as long as you require. Then, work back along the row crossing over these first stitches, by bringing up the needle at M, down at N, up to O, down at P, and so on, until all the stitches have been crossed.

A second method is to work each cross stitch in full as you go. For one stitch, following the diagram, bring the needle up at K, down at L, up at M and down at N.

Fasten off in the back of the stitching.

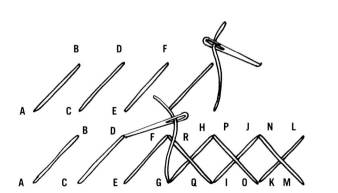

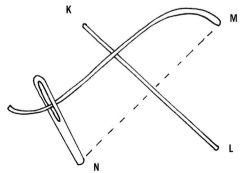

Detached chain

This stitch is suitable for working flowers and leaves. Working a short stitch produces a rounded shape and a longer stitch produces a narrower oval shape.

Bring the needle up through from the back of the fabric (A). Take the needle down as close as possible to the same point (B), making a stitch the length required (C). Pull the thread through, making sure that the loop is under the needle. Take a small stitch over the loop to secure (D).

Once complete, fasten off in the back of the stitching.

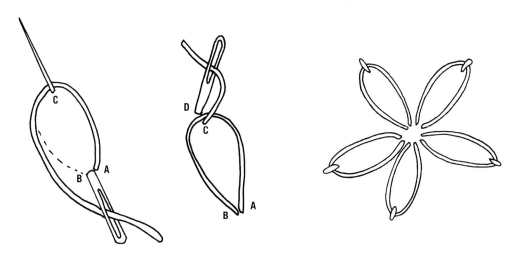

French knot

This stitch can be used alone or clustered together. Bring the needle through from the back of the fabric and wind the thread once around the needle.

Next, take the point of the needle back through the fabric very close to where the thread was brought through to the front.

Draw the thread through to the back of the fabric. Once complete this will form a neat, compact knot.

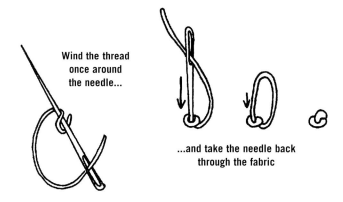

Wind the thread once around the needle...

...and take the needle back through the fabric

Hemstitch

Fasten the thread on by running the needle through the fabric beside the withdrawn threads.

Pass the needle through, two threads above the withdrawn threads and behind four threads. Pass the needle behind the same four threads again, and pull them together. Continue along the required length.

Repeat to the other side of the withdrawn threads, pulling together the same four threads for the simple pattern.

For a zigzag effect, pull together two threads from one group and two from the next.

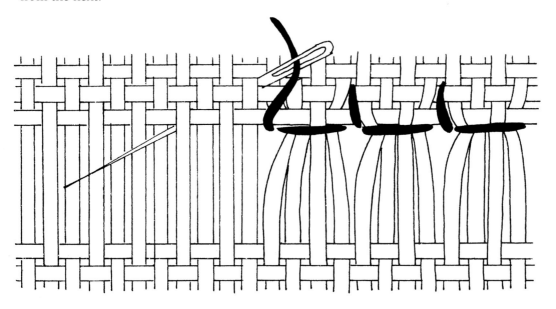

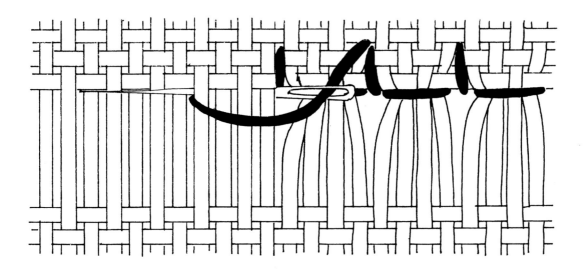

Running stitch

This stitch is basically the same as darning, but can be worked on a plain fabric or as a counted thread technique.

The needle is simply taken in and out of the fabric to form the line or shape required.

If the stitch is used for quilting, a smaller stitch can be obtained by stab stitching. Take the needle through the fabrics and draw the thread through. Then, in a second movement, bring the needle and thread back through the fabrics again. Each stitch is worked in two movements.

For double running stitch, create a row of return stitches which alternate between the first stitches.

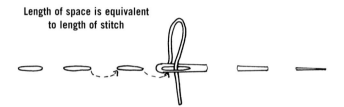

**Length of space is equivalent
to length of stitch**

Seeding stitches

Seeding is an effect created by stitching short straight stitches in a scattered fashion at various angles.

Traditionally, two stitches were used side by side, although for those doing miniature work, one would be sufficient to produce the same effect.

Straight stitch

This stitch can be any length and used for tiny leaves or flowers. It can be used side by side, or angled to radiate. Bring the needle through from the back of the fabric and make a stitch to the required length.

Tent stitch

This stitch is used on an evenweave fabric or canvas. By using tent stitch, rather than half cross stitch, the stitches can be worked in any direction and will look exactly the same on the front. Tent stitch also prevents the thread from slipping behind the weave of the fabric and disappearing. The stitches can slope in either direction.

The top diagram, below, shows the placing of the needle.

The numbered diagram, below, gives the sequence for different directions. Bring the needle up through the odd numbers and take the needle back down through the even numbers.

When rows are worked next to one another, the same holes are used as the previous row; do not leave a thread of canvas empty between.

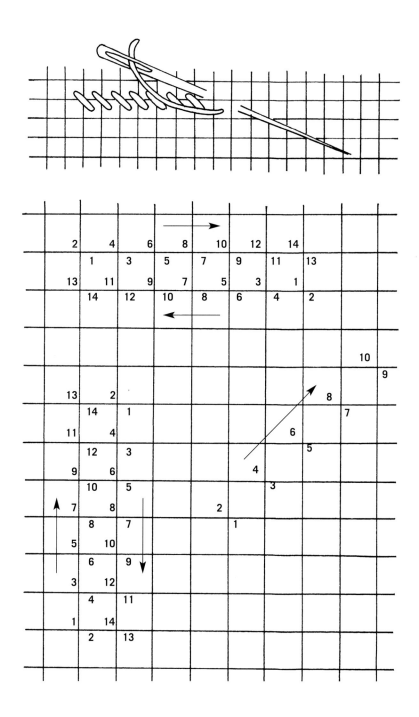

PROJECTS

Favourite
Flowers

Fig 4.1 Purse and pincushion on linen canvas, worked with silk and silver thread. English, 1600–25, Victoria and Albert Museum, London.

One of the most popular methods of embroidering flowers during the reign of Elizabeth I was in the form of 'slips', small pieces of canvaswork showing the plant motif as a cutting: often in bud, flower and fruit or seed at the same time.

The motif was worked on a piece of fine canvas using cross or tent stitch in different-coloured silk threads. The completed motif was then cut out, following the intricate outline, and applied to a silk or velvet background, the edge couched with silk or metal thread. By using this method, working small pieces on canvas at a time, the embroiderer was able to assemble large items such as bed hangings more efficiently.

As the designs were usually taken from herbals, the flower motifs are naturalistic and instantly recognizable (see Fig 4.1). The motifs selected for the projects in this chapter are based on examples held by the Victoria and Albert Museum, London, and Traquair House, Innerleithen, Peeblesshire, Scotland. (See my sketches of motifs on page 6.)

Any single motif or combination of motifs may be chosen for the items simply by selecting the appropriate chart. To make this easier, the thread colours required for each chart have been listed separately.

Each square on the chart represents one thread of canvas or one square block of threads on Aida fabric. If, for your own purpose, you choose to use an evenweave fabric, each square on the chart represents two threads of the fabric.

Tip

Dry cleaning or careful surface cleaning is highly recommended for all canvaswork or silk items.

Green Silk
Cushion

This striking silk cushion includes all the motifs shown in the charts provided to create a highly decorative cushion with folded, pointed edges on each side.

Materials

Interlock single thread canvas: 18 count, 60cm (24in) square

Back and trimming: either silk, cotton or lightweight furnishing fabric, 1m (39in) square

Interlining: cotton or calico, 50cm (20in) square

Zip fastener: 35cm (14in) long

Cushion pad: 41cm (16in) square

Stranded cottons as listed in the colour key: 4 skeins black, 6 skeins to match fabric and 1 skein each of all other colours

Sewing thread to match ground fabric

Size

41cm (16in) square

Working method

1 Cut the canvas into four equal pieces, each approximately 20cm (8in) square, and place into a rectangular embroidery frame. It is essential to use interlock canvas for this design; the weave allows the canvas to be cut to shape without fraying.

2 Using the relevant chart (Figs 4.2a, b, c and d), mark the vertical and horizontal centres of the canvas with a line of stitches using tacking cotton.

3 Complete all the motifs in tent stitch, using three strands of stranded cotton in black, and four strands of all other colours. You may find it easier to work the black outline first and then fill in the colours.

Remember that each motif is to be cut out, so avoid taking the thread across the back from one point to another, where an area will be cut out at a later stage. At this stage, do not embroider the insect legs, etc. These should be worked after the piece has been applied.

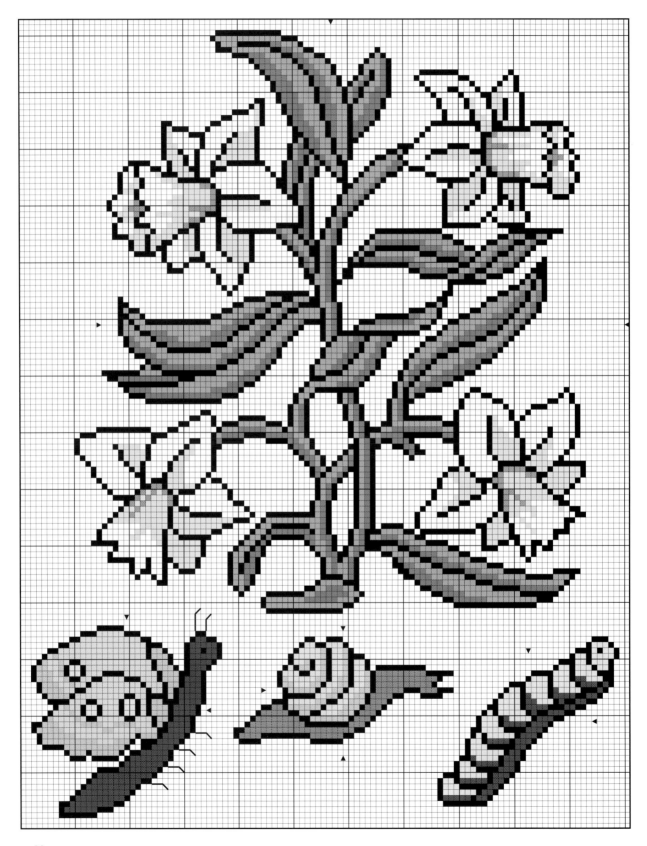

Fig 4.2a Chart for the daffodil and creatures (facing opposite).

		Skeins	DMC	Anchor	Madeira
Daffodil					
██	Black	1	310	0403	black
██	Light green	1	320	0215	1311
██	Dark green	1	319	0217	1313
	Pale yellow	1	3078	0292	0102
██	Bright yellow	1	444	0291	0105
██	Orange	1	741	0314	0201
Butterfly					
██	Black	1	310	0403	black
██	Dull green	1	3011	0845	1607
██	Light brown	1	841	0377	1911
██	Yellow	1	743	0305	0113
██	Very light blue	1	813	0140	1013
Snail					
██	Black	1	310	0403	black
██	Medium brown	1	435	0369	2010
██	Light tan	1	437	0367	2012
██	Pale peach	1	951	0376	2308
Caterpillar					
██	Black	1	310	0403	black
██	Pale green	1	3013	0842	1605
██	Medium green	1	3011	0845	1607

Applying the motifs to the cushion front

1 Cut out the ground fabric as follows: one piece 50cm (20in) square for the cushion front, one piece 43 × 50cm (17 × 20in), one piece 13 × 50cm (5 × 20in), and the remainder in 5cm (2in) wide strips (see Fig 4.3, page 36).

2 Press the fabric and interlining carefully to remove any creases, then position the cushion front over the cotton interlining.

3 Mark the cushion front with tacking lines as indicated through both fabrics (see Fig 4.4, page 36).

4 Mount the cushion front into an embroidery frame.

5 Carefully cut around the embroidered motifs leaving two threads of canvas all around the edges. Place into position on the diagonal lines and pin.

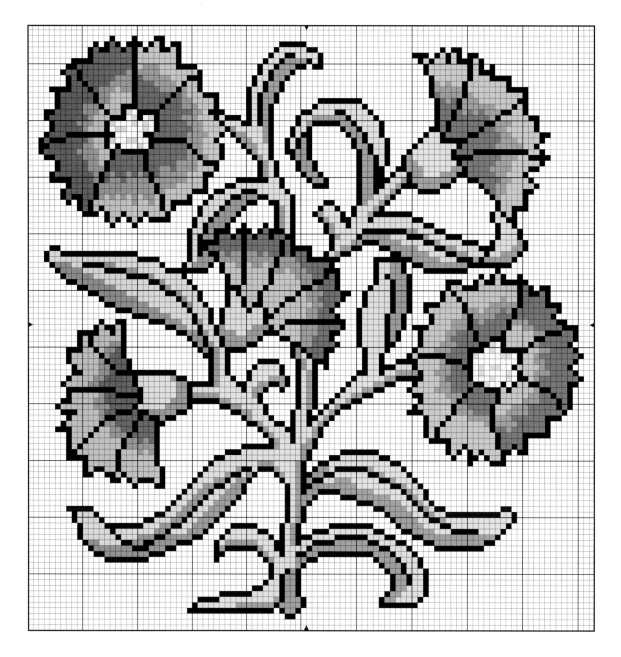

Fig 4.2b Chart for the pink or gillyflower.

Fig 4.2c Chart for the colombine and insects (facing opposite).

Pink or gillyflower

		Skeins	DMC	Anchor	Madeira
▉	Black	1	310	0403	black
	Light grey green	1	504	0875	1701
	Dark grey green	1	502	0876	1703
	Dark pink	1	891	035	0411
	Medium pink	1	893	027	0413
	Light pink	1	605	050	0613
	Yellow	1	743	0305	0113
	Pale yellow	1	3078	0292	0102

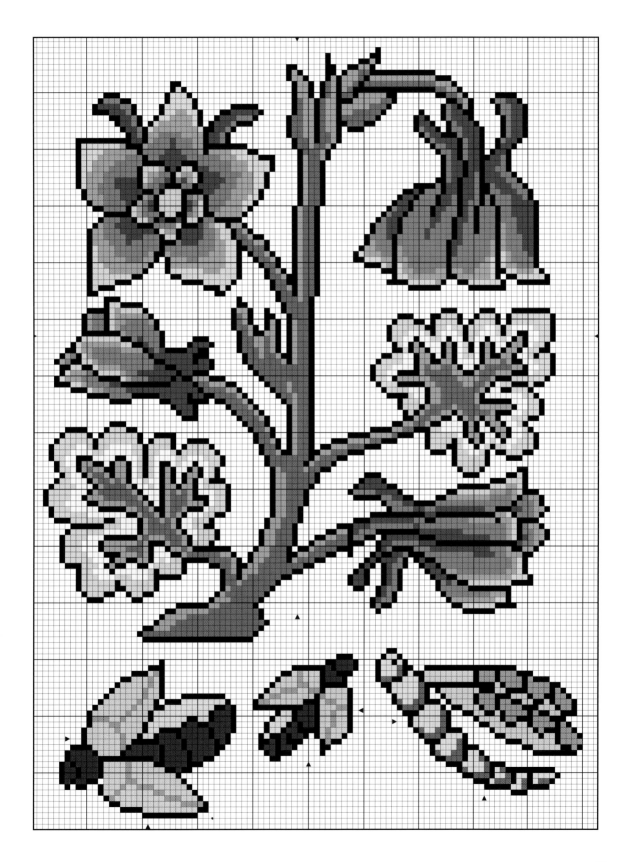

Colombine

		Skeins	DMC	Anchor	Madeira
	Black	1	310	0403	black
	Pale blue	1	827	0128	1014
	Light blue	1	799	0130	0910
	Medium blue	1	798	0131	0911
	Dark blue	1	820	0134	0904
	Light green	1	470	0267	1410
	Dark green	1	937	0268	1504
	Pale yellow	1	3078	0292	0102
	Dark Yellow	1	725	0297	0106

Bees

		Black	1	310	0403	black
		Pale peach	1	951	0376	2308
		Light tan	1	437	0367	2012
		Light brown	1	841	0377	1911
		Dark brown	1	839	0380	1913

Dragonfly

	Black	1	310	0403	black
	Pale peach	1	951	0376	2308
	Light tan	1	437	0367	2012
	Pale green	1	3013	0842	1605
	Medium green	1	3011	0845	1607

Briar rose

		Skeins	DMC	Anchor	Madeira
	Black	1	310	0403	black
	Dark rose pink	1	899	053	0609
	Pale rose pink	1	818	048	0608
	Yellow	1	743	0305	0113
	Light green	1	470	0267	1410
	Dark green	1	937	0268	1504

Fig 4.2d Chart for the briar rose.

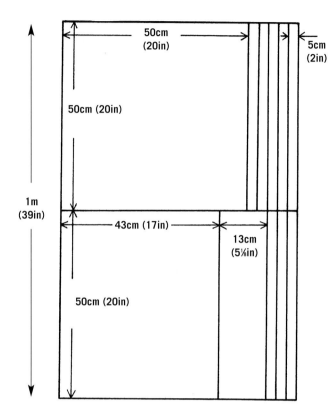

6 Using the narrow border of canvas around the edge, stitch each motif closely using polyester sewing thread (see Fig 4.5a).

7 Cover the edges with a smooth couched line, laying twelve threads of stranded cotton in the colour that matches the fabric (two sets of six threads laid side by side). Ensure that the strands lay flat and do not twist. Stitch down with two strands of stranded cotton, working the stitches at 2–3mm (⅛in) intervals (see Fig 4.5b).

8 Once complete, add the small details to the insects, such as legs, in backstitch using two strands of stranded cotton.

9 Remove all tacking lines.

Fig 4.3 Cutting diagram for the Green silk cushion.

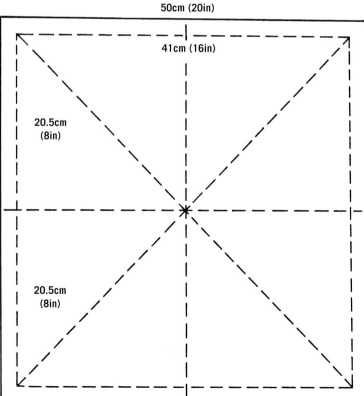

Fig 4.4 Marking the front of the cushion with tacking stitches.

Fig 4.5 Applying the canvaswork motifs to the fabric.

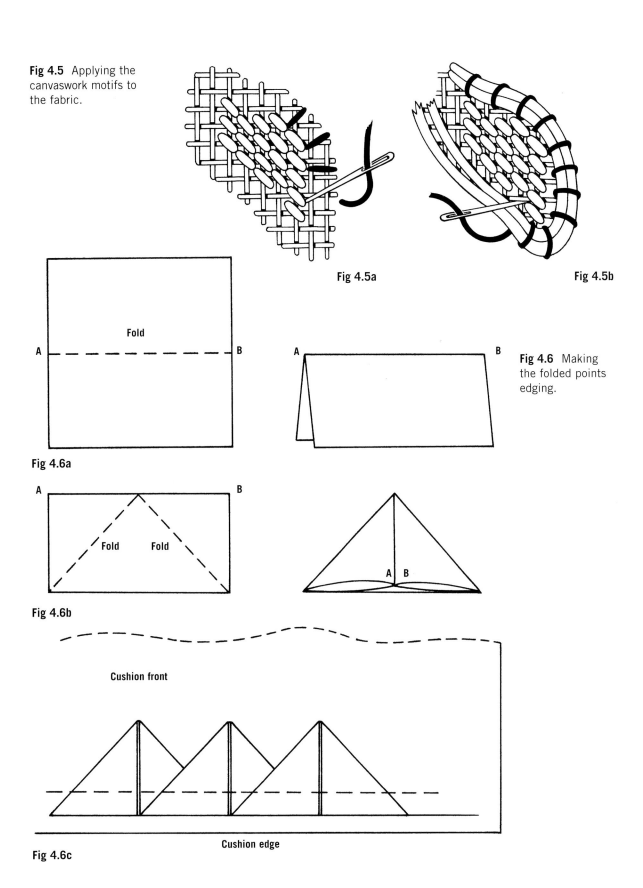

Fig 4.5a

Fig 4.5b

Fold

A

B

Fig 4.6a

A

B

Fig 4.6 Making the folded points edging.

A

B

Fold

Fold

Fig 4.6b

A B

Cushion front

Cushion edge

Fig 4.6c

Making the folded points cushion edging

1 Prepare as shown in Fig 4.6.

2 Cut several 5cm (2in) strips from the surplus ground fabric. Next cut the strips into 5cm (2in) squares. A total of 64 squares are required.

3 Fold each square in half along A to B and press with an iron (see Fig 4.6a).

4 Bring the two top corners down to the centre of the lower edge, to form a triangle, and press (see Fig 4.6b) .

5 Place the overlapping triangles along the edge of the cushion front as shown, with the raw edges to the outside edge and tack into position along the final sewing line for the cushion edge (see Fig 4.6c).

Making up

1 Prepare the back of the cushion as shown in Fig 4.7.

2 Place the two pieces right side together and stitch above and below the zip opening position (Fig 4.7a). Press the seam open (Fig 4.7b).

3 Insert the zip fastener (Fig 4.7c).

4 Partially open the zip fastener (to allow access when turning the cover through). Place the front and back of the cushion right sides together.

5 Stitch all round the edges of the cushion (see Fig 4.7d). Trim the raw edges to 1cm (⅜in) and zigzag or overlock the edge to prevent fraying.

6 Turn the cover through and insert the cushion pad.

Fig 4.7 Making the back of the cushion.

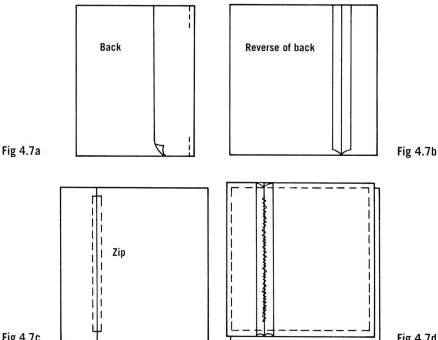

Back

Reverse of back

Fig 4.7a

Fig 4.7b

Zip

Fig 4.7c

Fig 4.7d

Cream Silk
Cushion

This cushion has a motif based on a sixteenth-century example at Traquair House, framed by a quilted border based on the popular strapwork design of the period. Any of the four charted designs can be selected for the central motif.

Materials

Interlock single thread canvas: 14 count, 23cm (9in) square

Silk, cotton or lightweight furnishing fabric: 1m (39in) square

Lightweight cotton interlining: 0.5m × 1m (20in × 39in) wide

Wadding: (2oz), 50cm (20in) square

Sewing thread to match the cushion fabric

Zip fastener: 35cm (14in)

Piping cord: 2.5m (96in)

Cushion pad: 41cm (16in)

Tracing and tissue paper

Stranded cotton as listed in the colour key: 3 skeins black, 1 skein other colours and 1 skein to match fabric

Size

41cm (16in) square

Working method

1 Mount the canvas in a small square embroidery frame.
2 Refer to the desired chart (Figs 4.2a, b, c or d), and work the main motif on interlock canvas in tent stitch. Mark the vertical and horizontal centres of the canvas with a line of tacking stitches. Begin by working the black outlines first using three strands of black and six strands for the colours. Do not take the threads across the back of the work.
3 Complete the motif.

Applying the motif

1 Cut out the cushion fabric as shown in Fig 4.8: one piece 50cm (20in) square (front of cushion), one piece 43 × 50cm (17 × 20in), one piece 13 × 50cm (5 × 20in), and four diagonal strips 5cm (2in) wide.
2 Cut two pieces of interlining, 50cm (20in) square.
3 Press the fabric and interlining to remove creases and place the front of the cushion over one piece of the interlining.
4 Mark with tacking stitches as shown in Fig 4.9 opposite.

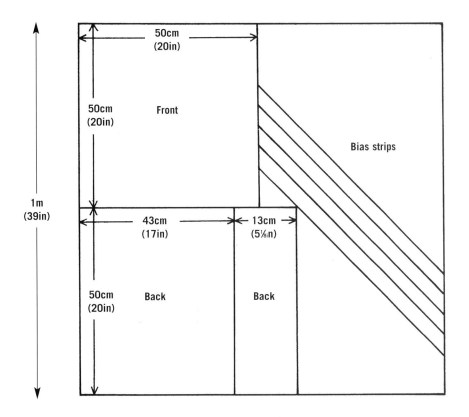

Fig 4.8 Cutting diagram for the Cream cushion.

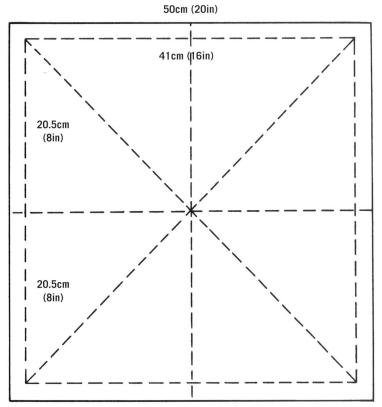

Fig 4.9 Marking the front of the cushion with tacking stitches.

41

5 Mount the cushion front into an embroidery frame.

6 Carefully cut around the embroidered motif to within two threads of canvas, and stitch onto the centre of the cushion front with polyester sewing thread (see Fig 4.5, page 37).

7 Once complete, cover the edge with a smooth couched line, laying twelve threads of stranded cotton in the colour that matches the fabric (two sets of six threads laid side by side). Ensure that the strands lay flat and do not twist. Stitch down with two strands of stranded cotton, working the stitches at 2–3mm (⅛in) intervals.

8 Remove all tacking lines.

Preparing for quilting

1 Cut away the surplus interlining from behind the cushion front to within 1cm (⅜in) of the applied motif. This reduces excess bulk before quilting.

2 Using a black waterproof pen and some tracing paper, trace the border pattern (see Fig 4.10) to size. The diagram shows one quarter of the border – reposition the tracing paper for each section until complete. Alternatively, photocopy the diagram four times and join them together.

3 Place the cushion front over the tracing or photocopy and, with a water-soluble embroidery pen, trace the design onto the fabric. The lightweight fabric should allow you to see through to the design. Before you do so, though, first test the pen on a spare piece of fabric to make sure that the line disappears when dabbed with water on a cotton bud. If it fails to do so (as happens with some fabrics or if the fabric watermarks), use the transfer method, as follows. This is also a good method if your fabric is opaque.

Trace the pattern on to tissue paper, and lay the paper over the cushion front in position and tack through the lines of the design and fabric, starting and finishing securely. Carefully tear away the tissue leaving the tacking stitches in place as a guide for the quilting.

4 Cut a square of wadding to the size of the cushion front, allowing an extra 4cm (1⁹⁄₁₆in) around the edge.

5 Place the cushion front on top of the wadding, with the remaining square of interlining underneath the wadding. Tack the three layers together as shown in Fig 4.11, page 44.

6 Using a small running stitch, quilt the border design through all three layers. Remove the tacking stitches as you quilt.

7 When complete, trim the wadding to the finished size of the cushion, but leave the turnings of the other two layers in place.

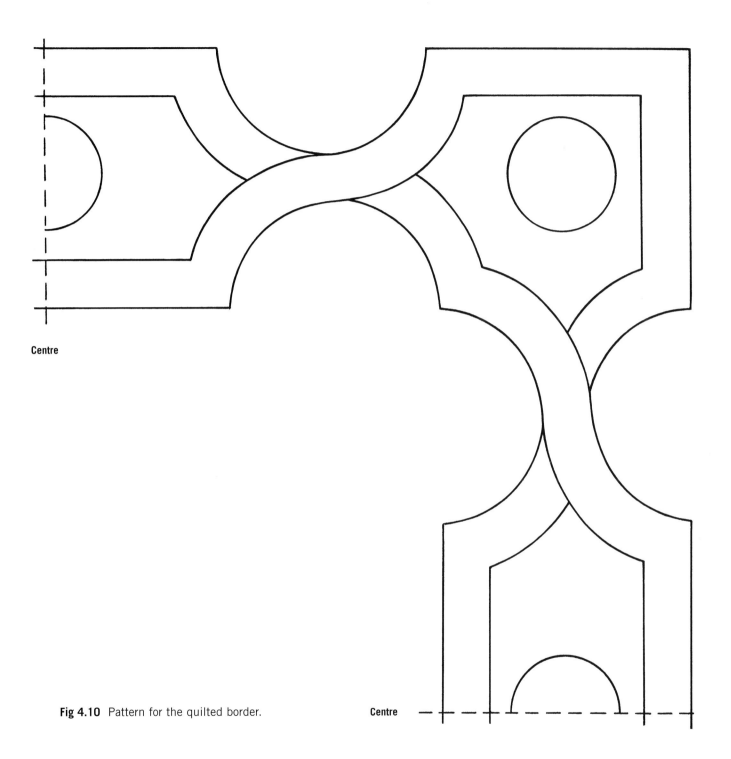

Centre

Fig 4.10 Pattern for the quilted border.

Centre

Fig 4.11 Preparation for quilting.

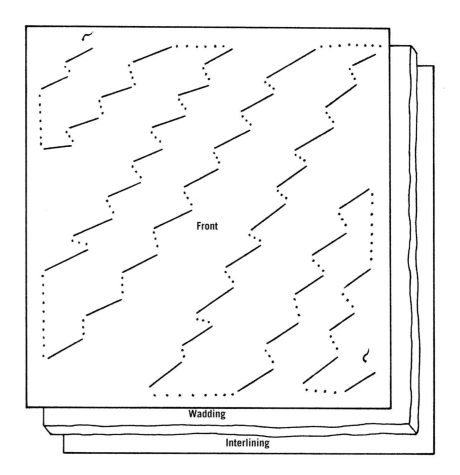

Making a piped edging

1 Cut bias (diagonal) strips from the surplus cushion fabric and join as shown in Fig 4.12a. You need a length of 2.2m (86in). Press seams open.

2 Lay the piping cord down the centre of the strip on the reverse side (see Fig 4.12b). Fold the fabric over and secure with running stitch or by machine using a zipper foot to place the stitches close to the cord (see Fig 4.12c).

3 Place the piping around the edge of the cushion front, with all the raw edges to the outside and tack or machine into position (see Fig 4.12d).

Making up

Prepare the back of the cushion and complete as for the Green silk cushion, shown in Fig 4.7 on page 38.

Fig 4.12. Making a piped edging.

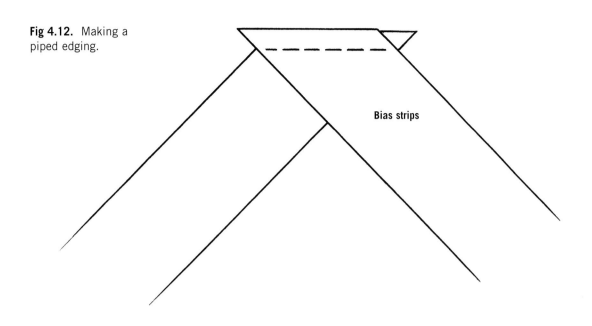

Bias strips

Fig 4.12a

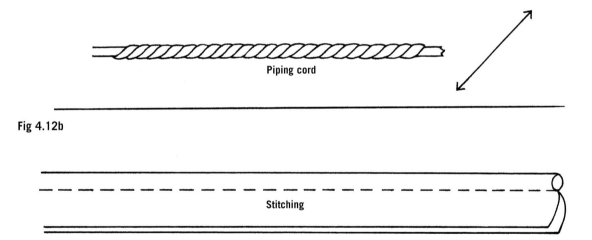

Piping cord

Fig 4.12b

Stitching

Fig 4.12c

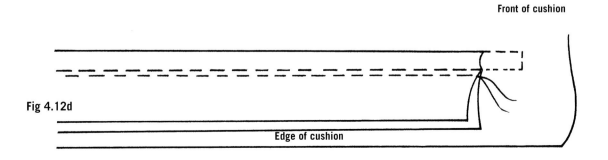

Front of cushion

Fig 4.12d

Edge of cushion

Silk Evening Bags

The slips for the two evening bags featured here have been worked on a finer canvas to make the motifs smaller. They are applied in the same manner as the silk cushions and outlined with gold metallic thread for added decoration. The bags can be embellished with beads or tassels as desired.

As with the cushions, any of the same four charts can be used. The choice of fabric colour will depend on the colours of the chosen motif.

Ensure that you use interlock canvas to allow the completed pieces to be cut out without fraying.

The Blue Bag

This dramatic little bag features pretty beadwork.

Materials

Single thread interlock canvas: 22 count, 15cm (6in) square
Silk, cotton or lightweight furnishing fabric: 0.25 × 1m (12 × 39in)
Heavyweight sew-in interlining, eg. Vilene: 0.25 × 0.5m (12 × 20in)
Sewing thread to match fabric
Beads for trimming as desired
Stranded cotton as listed in the colour key: 1 skein of each colour
Perlé cotton No 5: 1 skein of any two colours used in the motif
Imitation Japanese gold: 1 reel medium weight
Polyester sewing thread: 1 reel in old gold/mustard

Size

153 × 178mm (6 × 7in)

Working method

1 Mount the piece of canvas into a small rectangular frame.

2 Select the desired chart (Figs 4.2a, b, c or d), and mark the vertical and horizontal centres of the canvas with tacking stitches.

3 Using two strands of black and three strands in the colours, work the motif in tent stitch. Begin with the black outline and then fill in the colours. Remember that the motif is to be cut to shape so do not take any threads across the back of the work where a cut is to be made.

Applying the motif to the bag front

1 Make a paper pattern and cut out the fabric for the bag as shown in Fig 4.13. Two identical pieces are required for the front and the back, and two pieces for the lining.

2 Cut out the interlining to the exact size of the completed bag as indicated by the broken line shown on Fig 4.13. Two pieces are required.

3 Stitch a piece of interlining to the reverse side of the front and back of the bag using herringbone stitch (see Fig 4.14).

4 Apply the motif to the front of the bag and outline with two strands of metallic gold thread stitched with the old gold/mustard sewing thread (see Fig 4.5, page 37, and instructions for the silk cushions).

5 Turn under the side and lower edges and the top hem of the bag front and back, and tack into position. Secure carefully with running stitches into the interlining without taking any stitches through to the outside of the bag (see Fig 4.15).

6 Place a piece of lining on top of the wrong side of the front and back of the bag. Turn under the edges and hem into place just inside the outer edge (see Fig 4.16).

7 Using matching sewing thread, place the two completed halves of the bag together and ladderstitch the sides and lower edge (see Fig 4.17, page 52).

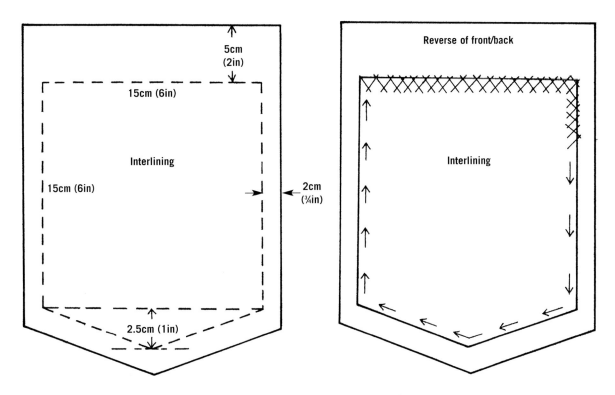

Fig 4.13 Pattern guide for the Blue evening bag.

Fig 4.14 Placing the interlining.

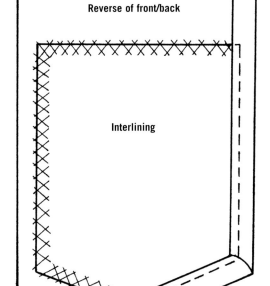

Fig 4.15 Turning the edges of the bag.

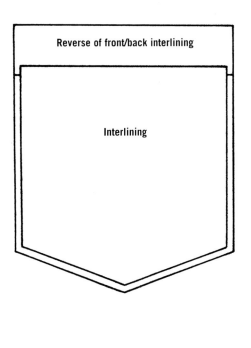

Fig 4.16 Lining the front and back of the bag.

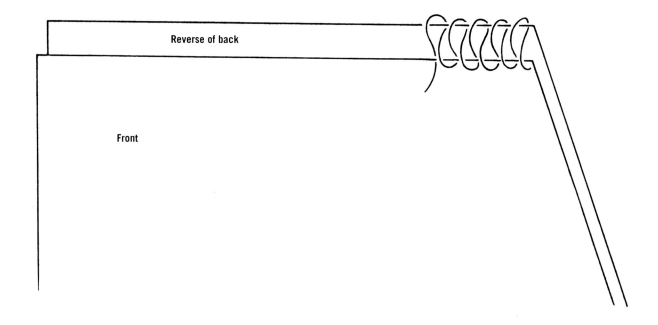

Fig 4.17 Joining the front and back of the bag using ladder stitch.

Making the cord for the handle and trim

1 Using the two coloured Perlé No. 5 threads and one of the metallic gold thread, make a plaited braid 150cm (60in) long (see Fig 4.18). Cut one thread of each colour and then one of gold, each to 325mm (140in) long.

2 Fold the threads in half and anchor to a pin, hook or tie to a door handle. Arrange the six threads into pairs by colour.

3 Plait by taking the outside pairs of threads in turn to the centre. Alternatively, make a machine whipped cord as follows, opposite.

Fig 4.18 Making a plaited braid.

Making a machine-whipped cord

1 Cut two threads of each colour and gold to the required length, plus 20cm (8in) to a combined length of 1.7m (68in).

2 Set your sewing machine to a wide zigzag, threaded with a thread matching one of the embroidery threads.

3 Pass each pair of threads under the machine, manipulating the zigzag to stitch them together. It is necessary to tension the threads by holding them taut between the hands, in front of and behind the presser foot, while passing them under the foot of the machine.

4 Next, join the three newly formed threads together in the same way.

5 Once the cord or plait is ready, stitch to the sides of the bag leaving a strap at the top to the desired length.

6 Decorate the ends of the plait or cord with beads. Additional beads can be added as desired as shown in Fig 4.19. Beads are arranged along the length of thread, one at a time, with a knot or small beads in between.

7 To secure the end, make a final knot and dab a small spot of PVA glue on it.

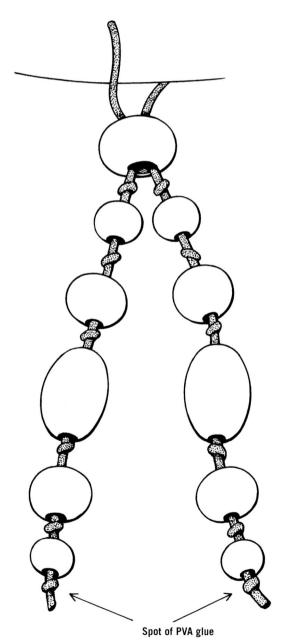

Spot of PVA glue

Fig 4.19 Making a beaded trimming.

The Pink Bag

This little shaped bag has a fold-over flap to enclose it.

Materials

Single thread interlock canvas: 22 count, 15cm (6in) square

Silk, cotton or lightweight furnishing fabric: 0.45 × 1m (20 × 39in)

Heavyweight sew-in interlining, eg. Vilene: 25 × 50cm (12 × 20in)

Sewing thread to match fabric

Beads for trimming (optional)

Stranded cotton as listed in the colour key: 1 skein of each colour

Perlé cotton No 5: 1 skein of any two colours in the key

Imitation Japanese gold: 1 reel medium weight

Polyester sewing thread: 1 reel in old gold/mustard

Size

178 × 165mm (7 × 6½in)

Working method

1 Cut out the fabric as indicated in the basic instructions for the blue evening bag, and following the cutting diagram (see Fig 4.20).

2 Cut one piece complete with a flap: the back of the bag.

3 Next, cut a second piece to A–B only: the front of the bag without the flap area.

Completing the bag

Fig 4.20 Pattern guide for the Pink evening bag.

Make up and trim the bag as for the blue evening bag.

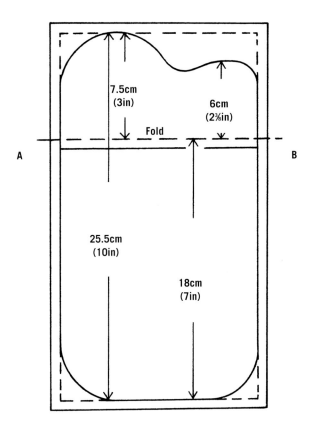

A

B

7.5cm
(3in)

Fold

6cm
(2⅜in)

25.5cm
(10in)

18cm
(7in)

Cross stitch
Cushions

The cushions featured have motifs based on items held in the
Victoria and Albert Museum in London, although you can use
any of the four charts, as before. The floral motifs are set within
decorative blackwork borders, one very simple and the other
more elaborate. The working method for both cushions is the same.

Materials

Aida fabric: 14 count, 50cm (20in) square in desired colour

Cotton fabric for interlining: 50cm (20in) square

Fabric for the cushion back: 0.75 × 1m (27 × 39in) wide in a toning colour

Sewing thread to match fabric

Zip fastener: 35cm (14in)

Cushion pad: 41cm (16in) square

Piping cord (optional): 2.5m (96in)

Stranded cotton as listed in the colour key: 1 skein of each colour

Size

41cm (16in) square

Working method

1 Mount the Aida fabric into an embroidery frame.

2 Mark the cushion front with tacking stitches as shown in Fig 4.21.

3 Work the blackwork border first. Select the chosen border from the chart (see Fig 4.22). Find the position by counting the squares on the fabric from the centre as indicated on the chart. Taking one strand of stranded cotton and using backstitch, begin to work the border from the middle of one side. Each square on the chart represents one block on the Aida fabric.

4 When complete, refer to the chosen chart (see Figs 4.2a, b, c and d, on pages 30–35), and work the main flower motif in the centre of the cushion in cross stitch using two threads. Each square on the chart represents a cross stitch over one square of the weave. As you work, ensure that all the stitches cross in the same direction.

5 Begin by working the black outlines, then fill in the colours.

6 Once complete, remove your work from the frame and place over the cotton interlining square.

Fig 4.21 Marking the front of the Cross stitch cushions.

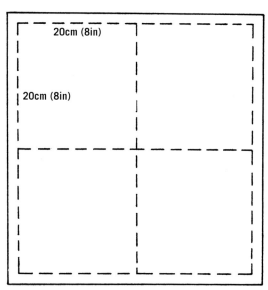

20cm (8in)

20cm (8in)

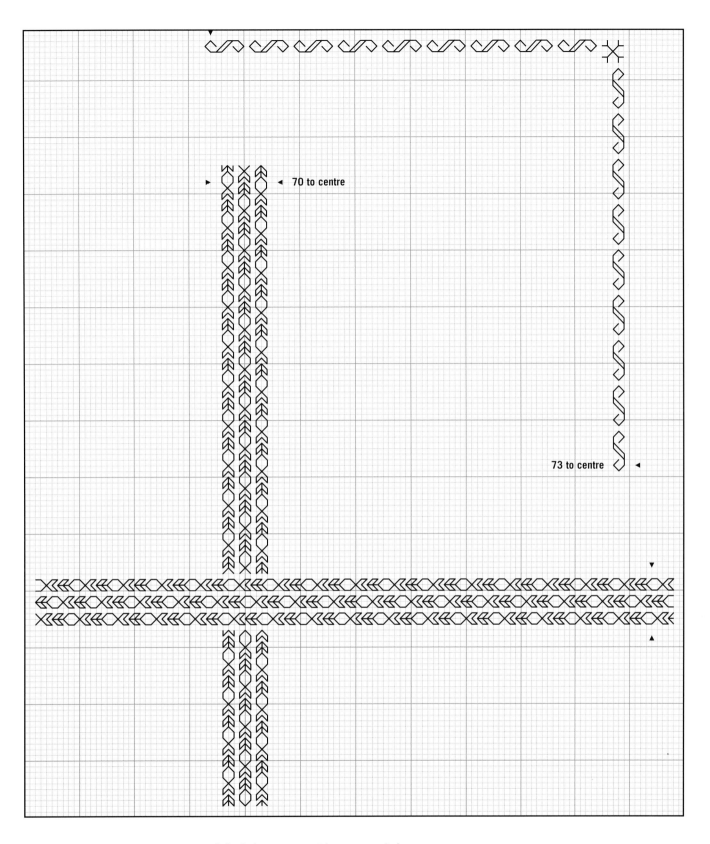

70 to centre

73 to centre

Fig 4.22 Chart for the blackwork borders.

Making up the cushion

Using the matching fabric to one of the colours in the embroidery, the cushion can now be made up in the same way as the green silk cushion, (see page 38). A piped edging can be added if desired.

An Embroidered
Picture

The motifs can be used singly or grouped together to form a decorative picture. I have used the rose motif, but you can choose whichever you like best. The motifs are embroidered into the desired positions but not cut out and applied as before.

The example shown has been worked on coin net, a 24-count cotton canvas. However, any evenweave fabric, Aida or canvas can be used, although the various counts will produce a variety of sizes.

Materials

Coin net: 24 count, 23cm (9in) square (or)

Aida: 18 count, 30cm (12in) square (or)

Aida or single thread canvas: 14 count, 41cm (16in) square

Stranded cotton as listed in the colour key: 1 skein of each colour

Size

200 × 180mm (8 × 7in)

Working method

1 Mount the fabric or canvas in an embroidery frame.

2 Mark the vertical and horizontal centres with a tacking line.

3 Refer to the desired chart (see Figs 4.2a, b, c or d, pages 30–35). Begin by working the black outlines, then fill in the colours.

4 If using coin net, use two strands of stranded cotton in tent stitch. There is no need to fill in the background. If using 18 count Aida, use one strand of stranded cotton in cross stitch. If using 14 count Aida or canvas, use two strands of stranded cotton in cross stitch. With canvas, the background will need to be filled in with either stranded cotton or crewel wool in a colour of your choice. Note that if the picture has been worked on 14 count canvas and the work has distorted, it may need to be blocked (see page 14 for full instructions).

5 Once complete, the picture can be framed with or without a card mount into a purchased frame.

Framing the piece

1 To form a backing board, cut a piece of card to the size of the inside of the rebate on the frame.

2 Cut a window mount from coloured mounting card to the same overall size, with a window cut to the desired position to fit the embroidery.

3 Place the embroidery into position on the backing board behind the window mount (see Fig 4.23). A small piece of masking tape can be placed at each corner to hold the embroidery in position. Place the glass or acrylic over top and fit into the frame. Seal the back with masking tape.

Fig 4.23 Preparation for framing the picture.

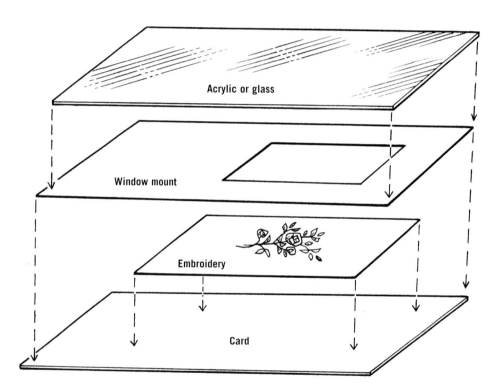

Acrylic or glass

Window mount

Embroidery

Card

Beautiful
Blackwork

Blackwork was a common embroidery technique during the sixteenth and early seventeenth centuries, and was used to decorate a wide range of items including covers, cushions and costume. Designs were diverse and included floral motifs, decorative edgings, all-over patterns and pictorial subjects. The scrolling stem formula was extremely popular, particularly on ladies' jackets, stomachers (a decorative panel of stiff material worn over the chest and stomach) and coifs (see Figs 5.2, below and 5.3, over).

Fig 5.1 A sampler of bands of pattern worked in Holbein stitch (double running), taken from *Double-Running or Back Stitch* by Louisa F. Pesel, 1931, published by B.T. Batsford: one of a series of volumes with charts and patterns inspired by seventeenth-century samplers. This sampler has been worked in a random dyed thread on an evenweave fabric.

Fig 5.2 Woman's embroidered coif (cap) on linen, worked with silk and silver-gilt thread. English, 1600–25.

Fig 5.3 Woman's embroidered jacket. English, 1600–25.

There were three main types of blackwork stitched: in Holbein and double running stitch (see Fig 5.4, facing opposite), speckling or seeding, and as decorative patterns. The embroidery was not always in black as the name suggests; it was often substituted with red, and sometimes blue. All three types of blackwork can also be found incorporating the use of metal thread.

Holbein or double running stitch was used whenever the work needed to be reversible – on a cuff or collar, for example. The pattern is followed initially with a running stitch, with alternate stitches missed out. The pattern was then completed by returning with a running stitch that filled the remaining gaps to forming a complete line. By careful fastening on and off, the work looked virtually the same on both sides. The sampler (see Fig 5.1, page 66) illustrates this method. The patterns are taken from seventeenth-century samplers.

Speckling or seeding was employed when a design was inspired by a woodcut illustration; the shading on the woodcuts was achieved by cross hatching, which produced a speckled effect. The embroiderers would simulate this with seeding stitches; the closer they were worked, the darker the tone. Additional stitches, such as stem and backstitches, were used for lines. There are examples of this technique in many museums, particularly the Victoria and Albert Museum in London. They have a lady's jacket worked in red thread based on the scrolling stem design. It is interesting

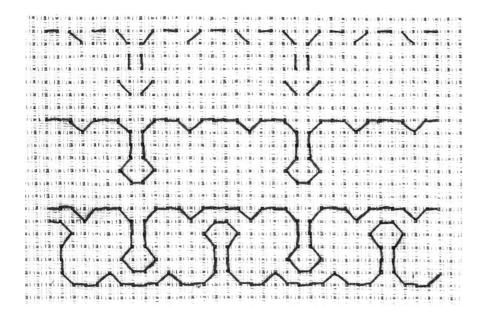

Fig 5.4 Working method for Holbein or double running stitch.

that the worker, to increase the effect of the seeding, has twisted a red and white thread together making the actual stitches themselves speckled.

Finally, highly decorative counted patterns were worked between the outlines of the design, with details in stem, backstitch or chain stitch. The Falkland pillows, a set of pillow and bolster covers, also in the Victoria and Albert Museum (see Fig 5.5), are a good example of this method.

Fig 5.5 Pillow cover with embroidered blackwork of coiling vines. English, circa 1600.

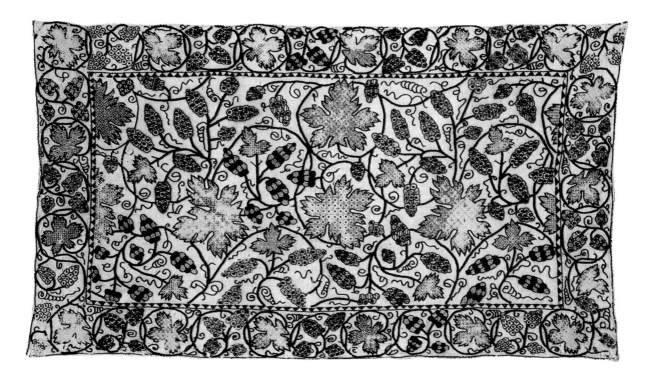

Table
Linen

A selection of borders, based on early patterns, have been selected for this project. They can be used for a wide range of items: table linen, accessories and clothing. The borders can either be worked directly on the items or on narrow bands of Aida fabric and applied afterwards. This is preferable when working borders for curtains, covers or tie-backs.

Fig 5.6 (top to bottom) Borders A, B and C respectively are adapted from sixteenth-and seventeenth-century sampler designs.

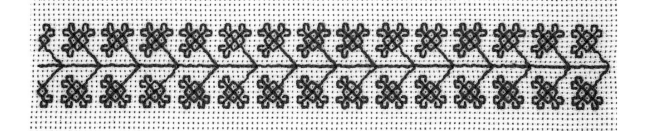

Each square on the chart represents either one square on Aida fabric or, if using evenweave, two threads of the evenweave fabric.

The borders can be worked using either double running stitch or backstitch with one strand of stranded cotton or coton à broder.

The following table settings use border motifs to decorate the place mats and coasters. The examples shown have been worked on evenweave linen with each stitch over two threads.

The quantity of fabric required and cutting layouts are given for one, two, four and six sets.

Materials

Evenweave linen: 28 or 32 count

1 set: 50 × 80cm (20 × 32in)

2 sets: 60 × 120cm (24 × 47in)

4 sets: 120 × 120cm (47 × 47in)

6 sets: 180 × 120cm (71 × 47in)

Stranded cotton or coton à broder in desired colour

Stranded cotton or coton à broder to match fabric colour

Tacking cotton

Tapestry needle No 24

Stitch count for borders

Border A: 1 repeat 20 × 19, motif 22 × 22

Border B: 1 repeat 16 × 16, motif 30 × 30

Border C: 1 repeat 21 × 16, motif 22 × 16

Size

Place mat: 42.5 × 32.5cm (17 × 13in)

Coaster: 13cm (5in) square

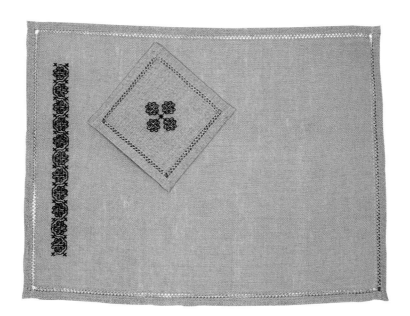

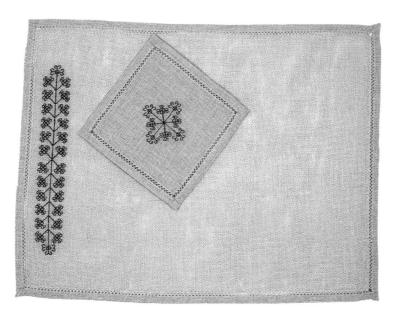

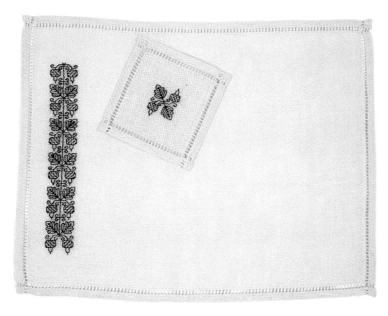

Fig 5.7 The three sets of table linen stitched with popular Tudor blackwork motifs.

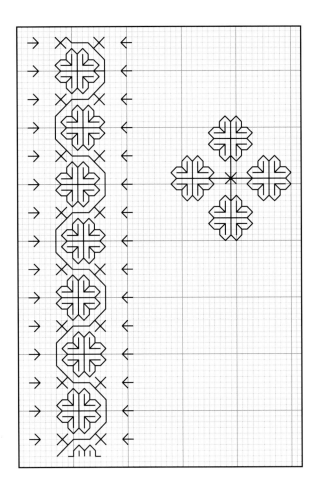

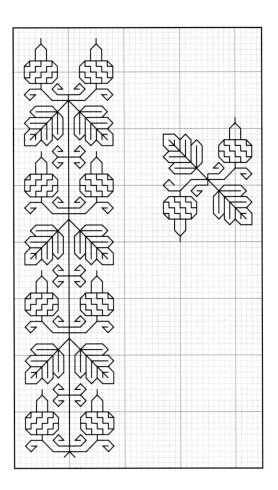

Fig 5.8 (clockwise, from top left) Charts for border and motifs A, B and C.

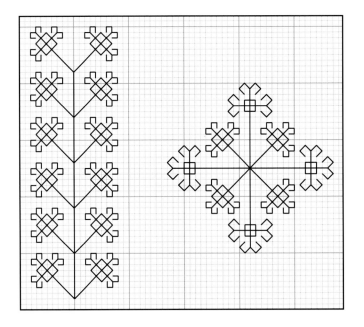

		Skeins	DMC	Anchor	Madeira
	Blue	1	820	134	0904
	Red	1	814	45	0514
	Green	1	319	683	1313
	Brown	1	898	360	2006

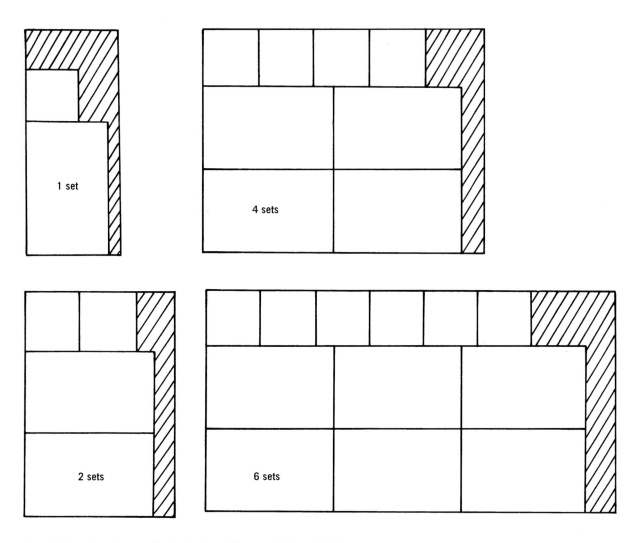

Fig 5.9 Cutting diagram for 1, 2, 4 and 6 sets of the table linen.

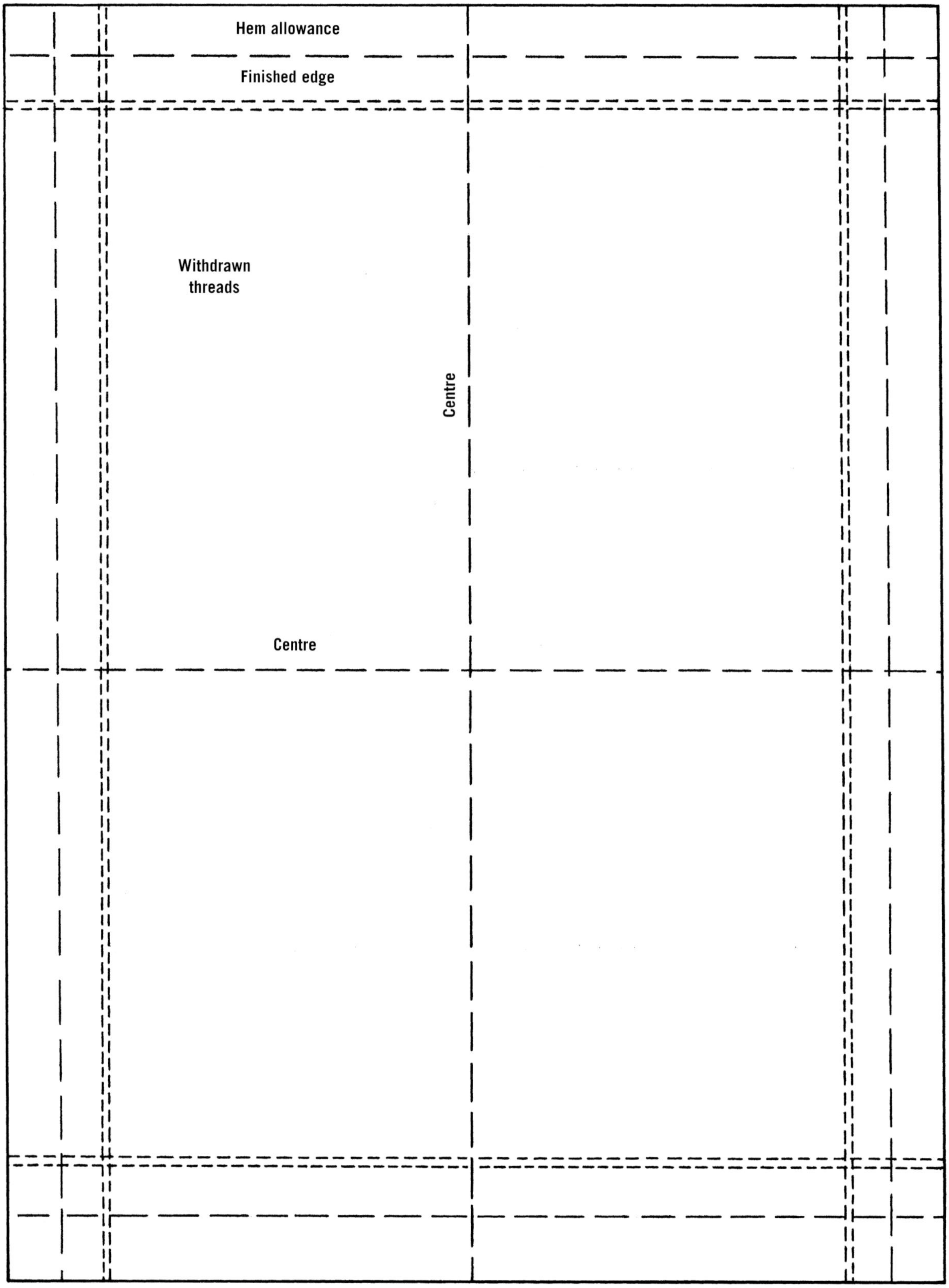

Hem allowance

Finished edge

Withdrawn
threads

Centre

Centre

Working method

1 Cut out the required number of place mats/coasters as shown in Fig 5.9. Cut out the place mats including a 6cm (2⅜in) turning allowance for all four sides.

2 Prepare each piece for hemstitching by running a tacking thread to mark the finished size, the broken line in Fig 5.10.

3 Also mark with a tacking line the vertical and horizontal centres (see Fig 5.10).

4 Measure in 1.5cm (⅝in) from the thread marking the outside edge, and withdraw five threads from the fabric weave, shown by the dotted parallel lines on Fig 5.10.

5 Prepare the hem to the reverse of the place mat/coaster. Trim the 6cm (2⅜in) turning allowance down to 2.5cm (1in). Turn under 1cm (½in), and then fold down again so that the folded edge is level with the slot of withdrawn threads (see Fig 5.11).

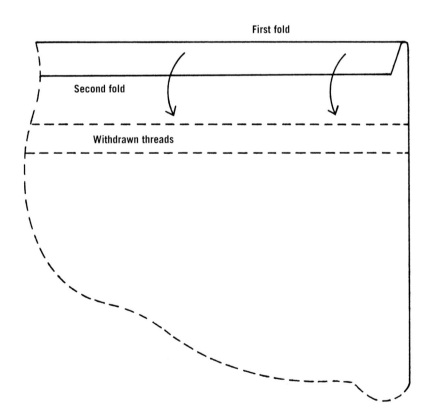

First fold

Second fold

Withdrawn threads

Fig 5.11 Turning the hem of the fabric.

Fig 5.10 Preparation of fabric for the place mats and coasters.

6 Mitre the corners (see Fig 5.12).

7 Secure the hem with tacking stitches.

8 Work the hemstitching, selecting the simple pattern with bars or the zigzag effect pattern (see Fig 5.13). The hemstitching will secure the turned hem.

9 Now select the desired pattern for the blackwork decoration from charts (see Figs 5.8a, b and c, page 74).

10 The border can be worked in double running or backstitch. Both will give the same effect on the right side of the work. The double running stitch will be neater on the reverse but will require more thought (see Fig 5.5, page 69). Begin initially with an advance knot (see Stitch Glossary, page 17), and thereafter fasten on and off securely in the back of the stitching.

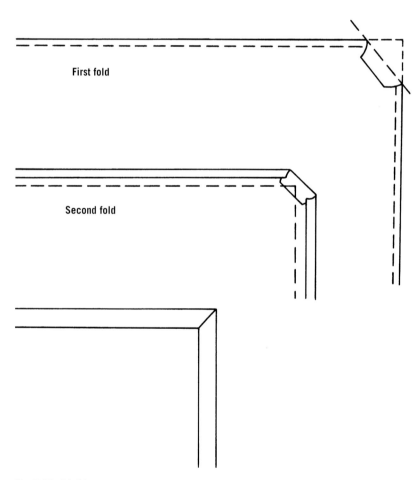

First fold

Second fold

Fig 5.12 Making a mitred corner.

11 Place the border 2.5cm (1in) in from one end of the place mat, or the motif in the centre of a coaster.

12 For the place mat, begin the border on the horizontal tacking line and work to the desired length above the centre. Return to the centre and complete the border to the same length below the centre line.

13 For the coaster, begin in the centre.

14 Press the finished item on the wrong side using a soft surface.

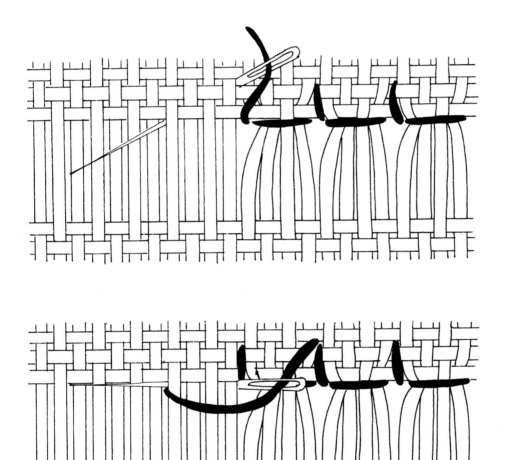

Fig 5.13 Hemstitching.

The
Banquet

This picture is based on an embroidered table carpet in the Victoria and Albert Museum in London, depicting Lucretia's banquet set within strapwork divisions filled with smaller scenes, fruit and flowers.

The project combines the use of blackwork with metal thread, a favourite combination in the sixteenth and seventeenth centuries. A little red has been introduced to enhance the detail.

This is worked on Aida, a block weave fabric. Each square on the chart represents one square of the fabric weave. Both backstitch and cross stitch are used. Work the backstitch in the direction indicated. If using an evenweave fabric, each stitch will be over two threads of the fabric.

Materials

White Aida fabric: 16 count, 41 × 35cm (16 × 14in) (or)

Evenweave linen: 32 count, same size as above

Stranded cotton or sewing cotton as indicated in the colour key

Stranded metallic thread in gold

Tacking cotton

Tapestry needle No 24

Stitch count

184 × 154

Size

29 × 25cm (11½ × 9¾in)

Working method

1 Prepare the fabric by marking with tacking thread the vertical and horizontal centres.
2 Mount the fabric into a rectangular embroidery frame (see page 11).
3 Begin the embroidery close to the centre, working towards the borders. Use a single strand of stranded cotton and two of the metallic gold. Do not pass a black or red thread across the back of the work, as this may show through the fabric once mounted.
4 When complete, remove from the embroidery frame.
5 Stretch the piece over a board and frame (see pages 16 and 64).

		Skeins	DMC	Anchor	Madeira
■	Black	1	820	134	0904
▨	Gold	1	814	45	0514
■	Red	1	319	683	1313

Fig 5.14 Charts for The Banquet.

Blackwork
Cushion

This pretty little cushion reflects the pattern of a simple knot garden as described in the next chapter. It is worked very simply in backstitch. The cushion has a frill around the edge in a contrasting fabric.

Materials

Aida: 16 count, 50cm (20in) square (or)

Evenweave fabric: 32 count, 50cm (20in) square

Contrasting cotton fabric for frill and back: 1m (39in) square

Stranded cotton, coton à broder or sewing cotton in desired colour

Tacking cotton

Tapestry needle No 24

Zip fastener: 35cm (14in)

Cushion pad: 40cm (16in) square

Stitch count

130 × 130

Size

200mm (8in) square

Working method

1 Mark the vertical and horizontal centres of the fabric with a line of tacking stitches. The fabric can be mounted in a rectangular frame, or use a small round frame and move the area that you are working as you progress.
2 Refer to the chart (see Fig 5.15, overleaf) and begin the embroidery in the centre, using one strand of thread and backstitch throughout. Each square on the chart represents one block on Aida fabric or two threads on evenweave.
3 Once complete, remove from the embroidery frame.
4 Cut out the back of the cushion and the diagonal strips for the frill using the cutting diagram (see Fig 5.16, page 87). The dimensions are as follows: one piece 35 × 50cm (14 × 20in), one piece 15 × 50cm (6 × 20in), and four diagonal strips 10cm (4in) wide.
5 Join the two main pieces, leaving an opening for the zip, and insert the zip as instructed for the silk cushions (see page 38).
6 Join the diagonal strips together by the ends.
7 Press the seams open and fold the strip in half lengthways.
8 Add a gathering thread throughout the length, 4cm (1%in) from the folded edge. Divide the length into four and mark with a stitch or pin.
9 Take the completed embroidered cushion front and, with a tacking line, mark the edges to the finished size, 41cm (16in) square.

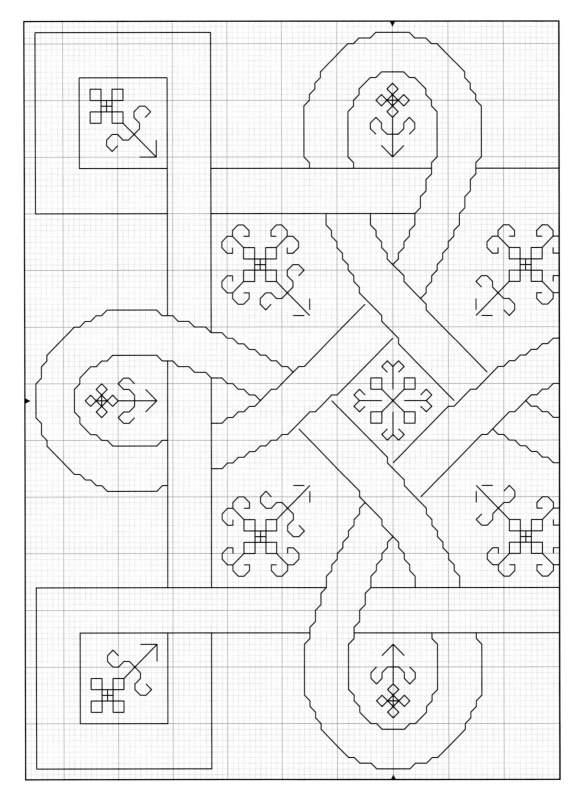

Fig 5.15 Chart for the Blackwork cushion.

10 Pin the four marked divisions to each corner of the cushion front. The folded edge of the frill is to the centre of the cushion front, with the raw gathered edges to the outside (see Fig 5.17).

11 Carefully draw up the gathering threads so that the frill is evenly distributed along each side of the cushion. Tack into place.

12 Partially open the zip. Lay the cushion back, right sides together on the cushion front. Pin or tack into position.

13 Machine stitch around the cushion on the line marking the outer edge.

14 Finally, turn the cushion through to the right side and insert the cushion pad.

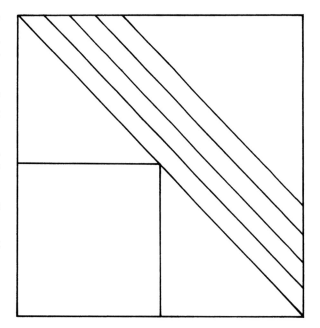

Fig 5.16 Cutting diagram for the cushion back and frill.

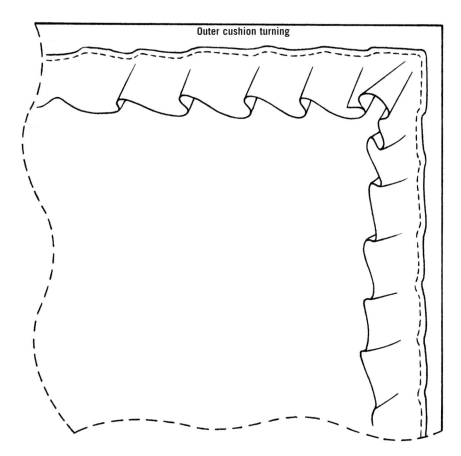

Outer cushion turning

Fig 5.17 Placing the frill.

Fragrant
Knot Gardens

During the sixteenth and seventeenth centuries the knot garden was a favourite feature of any sizeable household. The delightful interlacing geometric patterns of the knot gardens were reflected in the patterns featured by embroiderers to decorate many household and costume items (see Fig 6.1). Many of these patterns survive on spot and band samplers of the period on display in museums and historic houses.

In addition to being decorative, the knot garden played a vital part in the household as the 'medicine chest'. The gardens were planted with herbs which were used for culinary – but also predominantly medicinal – purposes. The fragrant herbs were also used to disguise the unpleasant odours resulting from the unsanitary living conditions of the time.

The importance of gardens increased over time as the interest in plant collecting grew with travel to far-off lands. The prestige of having discovered the latest exotic plant 'find' reinforced the status of a wealthy household.

The patterns characteristic of the knot garden have been used for this selection of projects, and for the blackwork cushion in the previous chapter (see page 84).

Fig 6.1 The knot garden at Villandry in the Loire, France.

Knot Garden
Cushion

The design for this cushion is typical of the interlacing patterns of the Tudor era. The interlacing effect is achieved here by using three toning shades of green, suggestive of shadows where the 'hedges' appear to pass over and under.

Materials

Aida: 14 count, 50cm (20in) square

Cotton fabric to match or contrast: 1m (39in) square

Stranded cotton as listed in the colour key

Sewing cotton to match fabrics

Tacking cotton

Tapestry needle No 24

Zip fastener: 35cm (14in) long

Cushion pad: 41cm (16in) square

Stitch count

133 × 133

Size

250mm (9¾in) square

Working method

1 Mark the vertical and horizontal centres with a line of tacking stitches.

2 Mount the fabric into a rectangular embroidery frame.

3 Referring to the colour chart (see Fig 6.2, overleaf), begin to embroider from the centre. Use one strand of stranded cotton and cross stitch throughout. Make sure that all the stitches cross in the same direction. Each square on the chart represents one block on the Aida fabric.

4 Once the embroidery is complete, remove from the frame.

5 Cut out the fabric and piping from the cotton fabric, making reference to the cutting diagram for the Blackwork cushion (see Fig 5.16, page 87). However, cut the diagonal strips narrower than for the frill: eg. 8cm (3in) wide.

6 Make up and insert the piping as for the Cream silk cushion (see Figs 4.12a, b, c and d, page 45).

7 Insert the cushion pad.

		Skeins	DMC	Anchor	Madeira
	Dark green	1	937	268	1504
	Mid-green	2	905	257	1412
	Light green	2	906	256	1410
	Pink	1	894	26	0414
	Mauve	1	554	96	0711
	Blue	1	799	145	0910

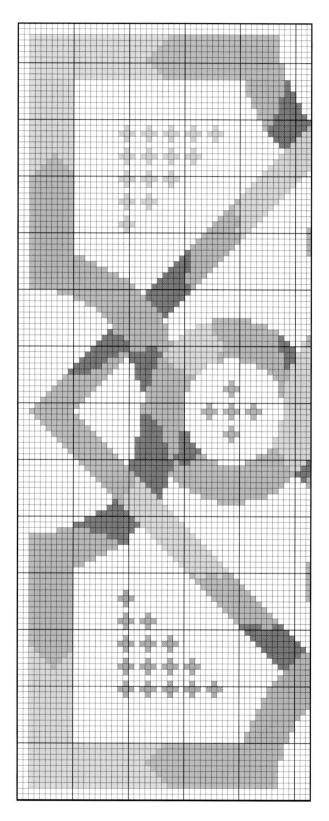

Fig 6.2 Chart for the Knot garden cushion.

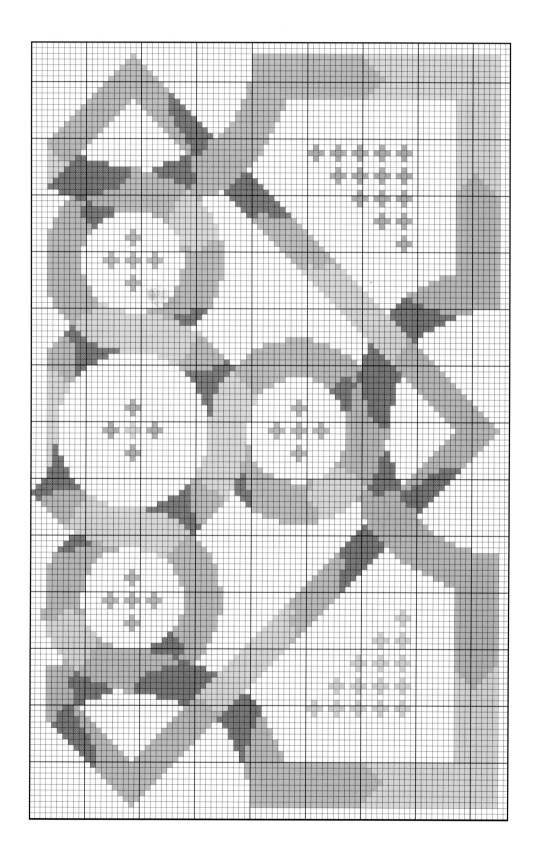

Embroidered Porcelain Boxes

These four porcelain boxes (widely available from craft or embroidery suppliers) are perfect for displaying the charming circular designs included in this section. The designs can be adapted to decorate a whole range of small items, and the patterns can be enlarged or reduced on a photocopier as required.

The projects are embroidered using a range of surface stitches or beads to fill areas within the designs. If enlarged, simply fill the areas with more stitches or beads than shown.

The making up instructions for the boxes are supplied by the manufacturer. Their original purpose was to display dried flower arrangements. When inserting embroidery, though, leave out the enclosed transparent cover as it sits awkwardly on the textured stitchery, which is shown to greater advantage uncovered. The embroidery will not get soiled as dust can be easily lifted with the nozzle of a vacuum cleaner.

Suitable fabrics for these projects – which should be smooth and lightweight – include cotton, silk and synthetics.

Design No 1

This design incorporates the use of metallic threads: imitation Japanese gold and stranded metallic thread. The former is couched down on the surface of the fabric with sewing thread, as described in the Stitch Glossary (see page 17). The stranded metallic thread is pliable enough to stitch with.

Materials

Smooth, lightweight fabric of choice: 20cm (8in) square

Selection of small beads

Sewing thread: old gold/mustard

Sewing thread: matching colour to fabric

Dressmaker's carbon or tissue paper

Embroidery or crewel needle No 10

Beading needle

Imitation Japanese gold, fine: 1 reel or skein

Stranded metallic thread: gold, 1 skein

Stranded cotton in colour to tone with fabric: 1 skein

Size

85mm (3⅜in) or as desired

Working method

1 Transfer the design on to the fabric using either method, as follows:

The dressmaker's carbon method

Dressmaker's carbon is available in packets of white, yellow, blue or red. Choose a colour that will show up on your fabric.

• Take a tracing or a photocopy of the pattern (see Fig 6.3, overleaf).

• Place the dressmaker's carbon face down on the fabric with the tracing or photocopy on top.

• With a sharp pencil draw over all the lines of the pattern, taking care not to move the pattern and carbon. (I keep an empty biro for this purpose: the hard point gives a good line.)

• Remove the carbon and pattern and the design should be clearly visible on the fabric.

The trace and tack method

• Place a piece of tissue paper over the pattern (see Fig 6.3). Using a pencil, trace the pattern on to the tissue paper.
• Lay the tissue tracing over the fabric in the desired position using tacking cotton, stitch through all the lines of the pattern working through the paper and fabric. Fasten on and off securely.
• Next, carefully tear away the paper, leaving the stitches marking the pattern on the fabric. For the position of the stitches, refer to the photo on the previous page.

2 Once you have transferred your design, place the fabric into a small round embroidery frame (see page 13). Using the Japanese gold double, couch the three circles first. Refer to the Stitch Glossary (see page 17) for starting and finishing threads.
3 Add the bars that join the circles.
4 Next, using the beading needle, add the clusters of beads in a sewing thread that co-ordinates with the fabric.
5 Using two strands of the stranded metallic thread, work a circle of detached chain stitches.
6 Continue with the sections of French knots and straight stitches.
7 Finally, complete the remaining segments with outlines of French knots in stranded cotton and metallic thread (see the Stitch Glossary, page 20).
8 Make up the item.

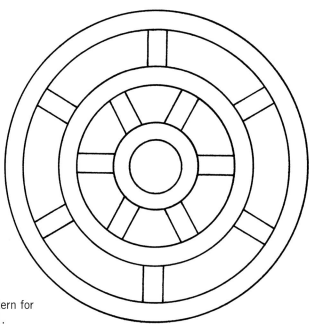

Fig 6.3 Pattern for Design No 1.

Design No 2

This design is worked in a selection of three complementary beads: glass or metallic are equally effective. Any small beads will produce a pleasing result.

Materials

Smooth lightweight fabric of choice: 15cm (6in) square

Sewing thread to match fabric

Small beads: three co-ordinating colours

Dressmaker's carbon or tissue paper

Beading needle

Size

70mm (2¾in) or as desired

Working method

1 Transfer the pattern (see Fig 6.4) to fabric using one of the methods described in step 1 for Design No 1 (see page 97).

2 Mount the fabric into a small, round embroidery frame.

3 Referring to the photo of the item, begin by stitching the selected beads to the outlines of the pattern, followed by a second row inside the shapes.

4 Next add the beads to fill in the centres of the main shapes.

5 Remove from the frame and make up the item as desired.

Fig 6.4 Pattern for Design No 2.

Design No 3

The shapes within this design are formed entirely with the use of French knots in stranded cotton. The surrounding 'paths' in the knot garden are filled with seeding stitches to provide a contrast to the raised knotted areas.

Materials

Smooth lightweight fabric: 15cm (6in) square

Stranded cottons as indicated in colour key

Embroidery/crewel needle No 10

Dressmaker's carbon or tissue paper

Size

65mm (2⅜in) or as desired

Working method

1 Transfer the pattern (see Fig 6.5) onto the fabric using one of the methods described in step 1 of Design No 1 (see page 97).

2 Place the fabric into a small round embroidery frame.

3 Refer to the photograph of the item, and begin by working two rows of French knots in dark green stranded cotton, using two strands, around the outlines of the main shapes. Work a single row around the smaller shapes.

4 Build up with rows of colour until the shapes are filled.

5 Finally, using the cream stranded cotton, fill the 'paths' around the filled shapes with seeding stitches.

6 Remove from the frame and make up item as desired.

		Skeins	DMC	Anchor	Madeira
	Dark green	1	319	683	1313
	Pink	1	335	38	0610
	Purple	1	550	102	0713
	Turquoise	1	807	168	1109
	Light blue	1	800	159	1002
	Cream	1	677	886	2207
	Yellow	1	444	297	0105

Fig 6.5 Pattern for Design No 3.

Design No 4

This tiny motif is the simplest of the designs and requires very little preparation.

Materials

Smooth lightweight fabric: 10cm (4in) square

Stranded cottons as indicated in the colour key

Embroidery needle No 10

Size

30mm (1¼in) or as desired

Working method

1 The pattern for this small design (see Fig 6.6) is so straightforward that transferring the design is not necessary. The starting positions, shown on the pattern, can easily be marked onto the fabric freehand.

2 Mount the fabric into a small, round embroidery frame.

3 Begin by using two strands of dark pink thread to work a French knot in the centre of the eight small circles.

4 Build up rows of colour around each dark pink knot.

5 Using the two olive green threads, work an area of detached chain in the central area.

6 Finish the item with some dark pink French knots or bullion knots on top of the detached chain.

7 Fill any remaining gaps with seeding stitches in dark green thread.

8 Remove from the frame and make up the item.

		Skeins	DMC	Anchor	Madeira
	Dark green	1	319	683	1313
	Olive green	1	471	255	1502
	Light olive green	1	472	264	1414
	Dark pink	1	602	63	0702
	Pink	1	605	60	0613
	Turquoise	1	807	168	1109

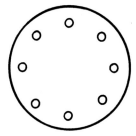

Fig 6.6 Pattern for Design No 4.

APPENDIX

Glossary of Terms

Aida fabric A fabric used mainly for cross stitch with the weave forming square blocks. It is available in various counts.

Bias cut The straight grain of fabric runs horizontally and vertically with the threads of the weave. To cut on the bias – or cross – the piece is laid diagonally on the fabric grain.

Blackwork A technique based on counting threads, traditionally mostly worked in black threads.

Canvaswork A generic term for all the forms of embroidery worked on a canvas ground, including Florentine work (see below). Canvaswork is commonly referred to as tapestry, but true tapestry is woven not stitched.

Chart A grid pattern, can be of coloured blocks, black and white symbols, or a mixture of both.

Coin net A cotton canvas in a 24 count, sometimes available in different colours.

Cotton A natural fibre used for fabrics and threads. Less costly than silk. Lightweight fabrics are suitable for miniature work.

Counted thread A series of techniques based on counting threads; including canvaswork, cross stitch, blackwork and pulled thread.

Cross grain (See Bias cut, above left.)

Evenweave fabric A fabric such as linen designed for counted thread work, woven with threads of an even thickness in both the warp and weft. Available in a wide range of counts.

Florentine work A form of canvaswork using straight stitches in a pattern of 'waves'. Also referred to as 'flame stitch': a descriptive term.

Interlining A fabric which is used to line the back of the embroidered fabric, especially on the inside of a cushion. Interlining can also be a special stiffening fabric used in dressmaking.

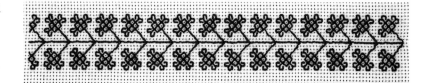

Interlock canvas A white, soft canvas with a special weave that allows the motif to be cut out without the canvas fraying. The weave is twisted in one direction.

Metal threads Originally flattened gold or silver-gilt wire wrapped around a core of silk, present-day metal threads are imitation foils. Their advantage is that they do not tarnish. Imitation Japanese gold is a smooth, shiny thread which is couched on the surface. Twists – as the name suggests – are multiple threads twisted together. Purls are coils of wire which are usually cut up and used in the same way as beads.

Opus anglicanum This means 'English work', the magnificent period of English ecclesiastical embroidery dating between the 13th and 15th centuries.

Prick and pounce A method of transferring a design onto fabric by pricking holes in the paper design, 'pouncing' with powder which passes through the holes and, finally, painting in the lines onto the fabric.

Pulled threadwork A white-work technique based on counting threads. The stitches are pulled tightly to distort the fabric and open the weave.

Quilting A method of layering three fabrics to create a padded surface. The layers consists of a top decorative fabric, a middle layer of wadding and a backing fabric at the bottom.

Raised stitches A series of textured stitches, including detached buttonhole, Ceylon stitch, French knots, raised chain and raised stem band.

Silk A natural fibre used for weaving fabric or for embroidery threads. Its fine, lightweight character make it especially suitable for creating miniature work.

Slip A gardening term for a cutting which has been appropriated into embroidery terminology.

Scrolling stem A term to describe the way the stem of a plant is manipulated to divide the ground of the fabric into different compartments to receive motifs.

Stranded cotton An embroidery thread of cotton which consists of six strands.

Wadding A full, fluffy fabric used for quilting or loose stuffing for toymaking, etc.

Sources of Information

Museums

Most large towns and cities have a museum with a display of decorative arts, which include embroidered items. Many cover social history, showing the way in which people lived and the artefacts they used in their everyday lives. Some museums will have authentic room settings with furnishings of a particular period. These provide valuable general information.

If you have a specific question, it is best to write to the curator in advance, stating exactly what you wish to know. A short list of clear questions will almost always bring a prompt response, but a general 'Tell me all you know about beds/chairs/Tudor houses/etc.' will rarely get a reply.

In most countries a list of museums and historical houses is published, usually updated every couple of years or so.

Libraries will have copies, or lists of their own, and sometimes a section devoted to local history.

The brief list that follows is a starting point, indicating museums which have collections of Tudor historical embroidery and, in many cases, furnishings.

United Kingdom and Ireland

The Embroiderers' Guild
Apartment 41
Hampton Court Palace
East Molesey
Surrey
KT8 9AU
020 8943 1229

Historical embroidery.

The Guild has branches throughout the UK and Ireland, the USA, Canada and Australia. Visits by appointment only.

Victoria and Albert Museum
Cromwell Road
London
SW7 2RL
020 7983 8500

Embroidery, costume and furniture.

Bowes Museum
Barnard Castle
Co. Durham
DL12 8NP
01833 690606

Embroidery, costume and furnishings.

Fitzwilliam Museum
Trumpington Street
Cambridge
CB2 1RB
01223 332900

Embroidery, mostly samplers.

Guildford Museum
Castle Arch
Guildford
Surrey
GU1 35X
01483 444750

Embroidery.

Maidstone Museum and
Art Gallery
St Faith's Street
Maidstone
Kent
ME14 1LH
01622 754497

Embroidery and furnishings.

Whitworth Art Gallery
University of Manchester
Oxford Road
Manchester
M15 6ER
0161 275 7450

Fabrics and furnishings.

Museum of Costume
and Textiles
51 Castle Gate
Nottingham
NG1 6AF
0115 915 3500/5555

Costume, embroidery and lace.

York Castle Museum
The Eye of York
York
Yorkshire
YO1 9RY
01904 653611

Room settings.

Hardwick Hall
Doe Lea
Chesterfield
Derbyshire
01246 850430

Tudor embroidery.

Blickling Hall
Blickling
Norwich
Norfolk
01263 733084

Textiles and embroidery.

Geffrye Museum
Kingsland Road
London
E2 8EA
020 7739 8368/9893

Room settings.

Royal Museum
Chambers Street
Edinburgh
EH1 1JF
Scotland
0131 225 7534

Embroideries.

The Burrell Collection
Pollock Country Park
2060 Pollokshaws Road
Glasgow
G43 1AT
Scotland
0141 649 7151

Embroideries and tapestries.

Ulster Folk and Transport
Museum
Cultra Manor
153 Bangor Road
Cultra
Holywood
Co. Down
BT18 OEU
Northern Ireland
01232 428428

Textiles and crafts.

Ulster Museum
Botanic Gardens
Stranmillis Road
Belfast
BT9 5AB
Northern Ireland
01232 383000

Costume and lace.

National Museum of Ireland
Kildare Street/7–9 Merrion
Row/Merrion Street
Dublin 2
Republic of Ireland
00 353 1 6777 444

Decorative arts and lace.

North America

Sixteenth- and seventeenth-century items may not be numerous. An enquiry in advance is advisable.

Note: many Canadian museums specialize in folk textiles, but may have small collections of embroidery.

Museum of Fine Arts
465 Huntington Avenue
Boston
Mass 02115
617 267 9300

Large collection of textiles.

The Art Institute of Chicago
Michigan Avenue at
Adams Street
Chicago
Illinois 60603
312 443 3600

Large collection of textiles.

The Brooklyn Museum
200 Eastern Parkway
Brooklyn
New York
New York 11238
718 638 5000

Costume, bedhangings and window hangings.

The Metropolitan Museum of Art
Fifth Avenue at 82nd Street
New York
New York 10028
212 879 5500

Costume and embroideries.

Philadelphia Museum of Art
Box 7646
Philadelphia
Pennsylvania 19101
215 763 8100

American and English embroideries.

National Museum of History & Technology
Smithsonian Institution
14th Street and Constitution Avenue
Washington
DC 20560
202 357 2700

Coverlets and embroidery.

Royal Ontario Museum
100 Queen's Park
Toronto
Ontario M55 2C6
416 586 5549

Large collection of embroidery and lace.

Historic houses

These houses are a good source of reference. Some will be restored to a particular era, but many have been added to over the centuries. Textiles, furnishings and embroidery are displayed within room settings.

In most countries there are heritage organizations to care for these estates and houses, such as the National Trust and English Heritage in the UK.

Books

Information and illustrations can be found in books on embroidery, interior decoration, restoring period houses, furniture and decorative art styles. There are many specialist periodicals available covering these areas. Your local reference library, or a browse in a large book shop, are good starting points.

The brief list which follows includes some books which may be out of print, but can be found at libraries or purchased from secondhand book dealers.

Artley, Alexander (Ed)
Putting Back the Style,
Ward Lock, London, UK, 1988
ISBN 0 7063 6708 1

Benn, Elizabeth (Ed)
Treasures from the Embroiderers'
Guild Collection
David and Charles, Devon,
UK, 1991
ISBN 0 7153 9829 6

Johnson, Pauline
Three Hundred Years of
Embroidery: 1600–1900
Wakefield Press in association
with the Embroiderers' Guild
of South Australia and the
Embroiderers' Guild, UK, 1987
ISBN 0 949268 81X

King, Donald and Levy, Santina
The Victoria and Albert
Museum's Textile Collection:
Embroidery in Britain from 1200
to 1750
V&A Museum, London,
UK, 1993
ISBN 0 85533 6501

Miller, Judith and Martin
Period Details
Mitchell Beazley, London,
UK, 1988
ISBN 0 85533 6501

Swain, Margaret
Scottish Embroidery: Medieval
to Modern
B. T. Batsford, London,
UK, 1986
ISBN 0 7134 4638 2

Vince, John
The Country House:
How It Worked
John Murray (Publishers),
London, UK, 1991
ISBN 0 7195 4769 5

Warner, Pamela,
Embroidery: A History
B. T. Batsford, London,
UK, 1991
ISBN 0 7134 61063

International suppliers

The following suppliers operate a very efficient international mail order service.

Borcraft Miniatures
Woodland
Bewholme Road
Atwick
Nr Driffield
East Yorkshire
Y025 8DP
01964 537722
www.borcraft-miniatures.co.uk

Stripwood and miniature
mouldings.

Wood Supplies
94 Colliers Water Lane
Thornton Heath
Surrey
CR7 7LB
020 8689 1865
Monday to Friday, 6–9pm

Stripwood and miniature
mouldings.

Campden Needlecraft Centre
High Street
Chipping Campden
Gloucestershire
GL55 6AG
01386 840583

Evenweave fabrics, canvas,
frames and threads

The Silk Route
32 Wolseley Road
Godalming
Surrey
GU7 3EA
01483 420544

Silk fabrics and brocades for
miniatures.

About the Author

Pamela Warner's interest in embroidery began in the mid-1950s with her studies for a National Design Diploma (NDD) in fashion – which included embroidery – at Bromley College of Art, Kent, in England.

After a career in banking and computing, followed by marriage and a family, Pamela rediscovered creative embroidery at an evening class. She went on to qualify and by 1979 was teaching embroidery for Bromley Adult Education and the Inner London Education Authority (ILEA). During the early 1980s she became involved as a tutor for City and Guilds embroidery classes at Bromley, specializing in the history of embroidery. She eventually took on full responsibility for the course. This continues to be her main occupation, along with working as an external verifier for the City and Guilds examination board. In 1999, Pamela formulated a syllabus for City and Guilds, enabling embroiderers to achieve a certificate in Miniature Embroidery.

Pamela began to pursue her interest in making dolls' houses and miniatures, including furniture and needlework. This led to writing books and magazine articles on the subject.

Pamela's work as a professional embroiderer has been exhibited widely, and she has undertaken many commissions for ecclesiastical and secular pieces. She has also spent many years restoring and conserving embroideries for Westminster Abbey and other churches and cathedrals.

This is Pamela's fifth book, following *Embroidery: A History, Miniature Embroidery for the Victorian Dolls' House*, and subsequent volumes *Miniature Embroidery for the Georgian Dolls' House* and *Miniature Embroidery for the Tudor and Stuart Dolls' House*, as well as a series of booklets on other aspects of embroidery.

Index

TITLES AVAILABLE FROM
GMC PUBLICATIONS

BOOKS

UPHOLSTERY

The Upholsterer's Pocket Reference Book	*David James*
Upholstery: A Complete Course (Revised Edition)	*David James*
Upholstery Restoration	*David James*
Upholstery Techniques & Projects	*David James*
Upholstery Tips and Hints	*David James*

TOYMAKING

Restoring Rocking Horses	*Clive Green & Anthony Dew*
Scrollsaw Toy Projects	*Ivor Carlyle*
Scrollsaw Toys for All Ages	*Ivor Carlyle*

DOLLS' HOUSES AND MINIATURES

1/12 Scale Character Figures for the Dolls' House	*James Carrington*
Architecture for Dolls' Houses	*Joyce Percival*
The Authentic Georgian Dolls' House	*Brian Long*
A Beginners' Guide to the Dolls' House Hobby	*Jean Nisbett*
Celtic, Medieval and Tudor Wall Hangings in 1/12 Scale Needlepoint	*Sandra Whitehead*
The Complete Dolls' House Book	*Jean Nisbett*
The Dolls' House 1/24 Scale: A Complete Introduction	*Jean Nisbett*
Dolls' House Accessories, Fixtures and Fittings	*Andrea Barham*
Dolls' House Bathrooms: Lots of Little Loos	*Patricia King*
Dolls' House Fireplaces and Stoves	*Patricia King*
Dolls' House Makeovers	*Jean Nisbett*
Dolls' House Window Treatments	*Eve Harwood*
Easy to Make Dolls' House Accessories	*Andrea Barham*
Heraldic Miniature Knights	*Peter Greenhill*
How to Make Your Dolls' House Special: Fresh Ideas for Decorating	*Beryl Armstrong*
Make Your Own Dolls' House Furniture	*Maurice Harper*
Making Dolls' House Furniture	*Patricia King*
Making Georgian Dolls' Houses	*Derek Rowbottom*
Making Miniature Food and Market Stalls	*Angie Scarr*
Making Miniature Gardens	*Freida Gray*
Making Miniature Oriental Rugs & Carpets	*Meik & Ian McNaughton*
Making Period Dolls' House Accessories	*Andrea Barham*
Making Tudor Dolls' Houses	*Derek Rowbottom*
Making Victorian Dolls' House Furniture	*Patricia King*
Miniature Bobbin Lace	*Roz Snowden*
Miniature Embroidery for the Georgian Dolls' House	*Pamela Warner*
Miniature Embroidery for the Tudor and Stuart Dolls' House	*Pamela Warner*
Miniature Embroidery for the Victorian Dolls' House	*Pamela Warner*
Miniature Needlepoint Carpets	*Janet Granger*
More Miniature Oriental Rugs & Carpets	*Meik & Ian McNaughton*
Needlepoint 1/12 Scale: Design Collections for the Dolls' House	*Felicity Price*
New Ideas for Miniature Bobbin Lace	*Roz Snowden*
The Secrets of the Dolls' House Makers	*Jean Nisbett*

CRAFTS

American Patchwork Designs in Needlepoint	*Melanie Tacon*
A Beginners' Guide to Rubber Stamping	*Brenda Hunt*
Beginning Picture Marquetry	*Lawrence Threadgold*
Blackwork: A New Approach	*Brenda Day*
Celtic Cross Stitch Designs	*Carol Phillipson*
Celtic Knotwork Designs	*Sheila Sturrock*
Celtic Knotwork Handbook	*Sheila Sturrock*
Celtic Spirals and Other Designs	*Sheila Sturrock*
Collage from Seeds, Leaves and Flowers	*Joan Carver*
Complete Pyrography	*Stephen Poole*
Contemporary Smocking	*Dorothea Hall*
Creating Colour with Dylon	*Dylon International*
Creative Doughcraft	*Patricia Hughes*
Creative Embroidery Techniques Using Colour Through Gold	*Daphne J. Ashby & Jackie Woolsey*
The Creative Quilter: Techniques and Projects	*Pauline Brown*
Cross-Stitch Designs from China	*Carol Phillipson*
Decoration on Fabric: A Sourcebook of Ideas	*Pauline Brown*
Decorative Beaded Purses	*Enid Taylor*
Designing and Making Cards	*Glennis Gilruth*
Glass Engraving Pattern Book	*John Everett*
Glass Painting	*Emma Sedman*
Handcrafted Rugs	*Sandra Hardy*
How to Arrange Flowers: A Japanese Approach to English Design	*Taeko Marvelly*
How to Make First-Class Cards	*Debbie Brown*
An Introduction to Crewel Embroidery	*Mave Glenny*
Making and Using Working Drawings for Realistic Model Animals	*Basil F. Fordham*
Making Character Bears	*Valerie Tyler*
Making Decorative Screens	*Amanda Howes*
Making Fairies and Fantastical Creatures	*Julie Sharp*
Making Greetings Cards for Beginners	*Pat Sutherland*
Making Hand-Sewn Boxes: Techniques and Projects	*Jackie Woolsey*
Making Knitwear Fit	*Pat Ashforth & Steve Plummer*
Making Mini Cards, Gift Tags & Invitations	*Glennis Gilruth*
Making Soft-Bodied Dough Characters	*Patricia Hughes*
Natural Ideas for Christmas: Fantastic Decorations to Make	*Josie Cameron-Ashcroft & Carol Cox*
Needlepoint: A Foundation Course	*Sandra Hardy*
New Ideas for Crochet: Stylish Projects for the Home	*Darsha Capaldi*
Patchwork for Beginners	*Pauline Brown*
Pyrography Designs	*Norma Gregory*
Pyrography Handbook (Practical Crafts)	*Stephen Poole*
Rose Windows for Quilters	*Angela Besley*

GARDENING

PHOTOGRAPHY

VIDEOS

MAGAZINES

WOODTURNING ◆ WOODCARVING
FURNITURE & CABINETMAKING
THE ROUTER ◆ WOODWORKING
THE DOLLS' HOUSE MAGAZINE
MACHINE KNITTING NEWS
OUTDOOR PHOTOGRAPHY
BLACK & WHITE PHOTOGRAPHY
BUSINESSMATTERS

The above represents a full list of all titles currently
published or scheduled to be published.
All are available direct from the Publishers or through
bookshops, newsagents and specialist retailers.
To place an order, or to obtain a complete
catalogue, contact:

GMC PUBLICATIONS,
Castle Place, 166 High Street, Lewes,
East Sussex BN7 1XU, United Kingdom
Tel: 01273 488005 Fax: 01273 478606
E-mail: pubs@thegmcgroup.com

ORDERS BY CREDIT CARD ARE ACCEPTED